THE COLONIZED EYE

Also by Joyce Nelson

The Perfect Machine: TV in the Nuclear Age

THE COLONIZED EYE

RETHINKING THE GRIERSON LEGEND

JOYCE NELSON

between the lines

Published by:
Between the Lines
394 Euclid Avenue
Toronto, Ontario
Canada M6G 2S9

Cover design by Goodness Graphics, Toronto
Typeset by FAX and Coach House Press, Toronto
Printed in Canada
Between the Lines receives financial assistance from the Canada Council, the Ontario Arts Council, and the Department of Communications.

CANADIAN CATALOGUING IN PUBLICATION DATE

Nelson, Joyce, 1945-
The colonized eye

Includes index.
ISBN 0-919946-90-9 (bound)
ISBN 0-919946-91-7 (pbk.)

1. Grierson, John, 1898-1972
2. Documentary films – Canada – History and criticism.
3. National Film Board of Canada.
4. Grierson, John, 1898-1972 – Views on politics.
5. Canada – Politics and government – 1935-1948.*
I. Title.

PN1998.A3G74 1988 791.43′092′4 C88-094449-8

For the peoples of Canada (from the Iroquois *ken-a-tah,* meaning "a cluster of dwellings")

We only become what we are by the radical and deep-seated refusal of that which others have made of us.

JEAN-PAUL SARTRE

Contents

Acknowledgements

I am grateful to the following individuals for their assistance and support of this project: Bernard Lutz, chief archivist for the NFB Print Archives in Montreal; Lyle R. Cruickshank, director of NFB Distribution Services, who arranged for archival screenings; Mireille Kermoyan and Rita Pecsi, of the NFB Communications Department; Connie Tadros, Susan Crean, and Sandra Gathercole, who gave recommendations for the project in its initial stages; the Dorothy and Oscar Burritt Memorial Award Committee, whose initial funding allowed for archival research. None of these people, for whose support I am grateful, is in any way responsible for the views expressed in this text, or for any errors that may be found, which are fully my own responsibility.

I am also indebted to Robert Clarke, who edited the manuscript and was very helpful in his suggestions, as always; to Linda Biesenthal for copyediting; and to the Between The Lines collective, who made its publication possible. As the reader will see from the plethora of footnotes, I am entirely indebted to the writers, scholars, and researchers whose works have preceded this one. In particular, it will be evident that I have relied on the ground-breaking work of Peter Morris, Forsyth Hardy, Elizabeth Sussex, and Gary Evans. I hope the reader will seek out these sources for further information. Finally, I am grateful to the people of Canada, whose support through the Explorations Program of the Canada Council and through the Ontario Arts Council, made further research and the writing of this text possible.

J. N.
August, 1988

Introduction

Appeasing the Ghost of Grierson

I have been for a long time interested in propaganda and it is as a propagandist I have been from the first interested in films.

JOHN GRIERSON, 1940

I began this work intending to document a particular phenomenon of Canada's wartime National Film Board (NFB), something that had fascinated me from the time I first heard about it nearly 20 years ago. In the middle of World War II, the newly instituted National Film Board, under the tutelage of founder John Grierson, had hired some 170 travelling projectionists to show films in rural communities, northern outposts, lumber camps, shipyards, factories, and trade union halls all across Canada as a way of promoting the war effort. To my knowledge, no other country ever attempted such a project on this massive a scale. It seemed an interesting subject for a book, one that might both illustrate Grierson's belief in democracy in action and inform readers about an unusual aspect of Canadian history.

The unquestioned assumptions with which I began my research in 1985 were all rooted in the Grierson legend: that he was a left-wing, populist film specialist with a strong belief in "the people first, the people above all" (as his favourite film from the war period, *The War for Men's Minds,* states); that his founding of the NFB challenged Hollywood's hegemony in Canada; that his internationalist vision was ahead of its time and a daring challenge to the powers of the status quo.

The deeper I got into the research, the more I recognized that what I was finding did not fit my original assumptions and framework. In particular, I began to see that Grierson was far more complex and enigmatic than his legend would suggest. In part, this was the result of my catching up (as a lapsed academic) with recent Canadian film scholarship, particularly the work of Peter Morris and Gary Evans. But also, I was finding significant contradictions and previously overlooked facts and connections that, to my way of thinking, raised important questions, especially about Grierson's role and impact in Canada during the six war years he was based here.

The research included the opportunity to view more than 60 of the wartime NFB archival films, which also challenged the basic premises of the project. At a certain point, it became clear that my intention to focus primarily on the wartime travelling projectionists' circuits, and to do so in a somewhat celebratory fashion, would be a distortion of the larger historical picture that was emerging for me. I would have to either abandon the project or expand the parameters of what I would write.

The decision to put forward this text, quite different from the one I had originally planned, was not easily made. I offer it in the spirit of trying to understand the past, especially the terribly complicated prewar and World War II milieu, which gave birth to so much of our contemporary legacy. My focus, however, is primarily on Canada and Grierson's impact during the war. Knowing that others are also re-examining the Grierson legend, and that there already exist several texts about Grierson with a quite different perspective, I assume that the interested reader has access to a variety of other views and alternative interpretations of events.

In what was probably the last interview he gave before he died in February 1972, Grierson urged Elizabeth Sussex, who was writing a book about the British documentary movement, to focus on something quite different from what she had planned.[1] Sussex intended to explore the subject through interviews using a very personal approach, concentrating on the achievements and reminiscences of the filmmakers involved in the documentary movement from the late 1920s through the immediate postwar era. According to Sussex, Grierson sent her a note after her interview with him, urging her to abandon that approach and to explore instead "the whole economic and political background out of which documentary had sprung".[2] Sussex admits that, because the suggestion was "absolutely characteristic of him", she did not follow it up.[3]

This book is a limited and partial attempt to do exactly what Grierson suggested. Ironically, it is precisely through exploring the economic and political background of Grierson's work from the 1920s through World War II that a very different reading of the man emerges. Perhaps on the eve of his death, Grierson himself was tired of his own legend. What I hope to show is that Grierson, at least until the end of World War II, was actually a champion of emergent multinational capitalism and that he used the medium of film as a public-relations vehicle to convey the wisdom and necessity of accepting the new economic order that would come to typify the postwar world. If this thesis is correct, then Grierson, long lionized by many in the postwar Left, must have felt admired for somewhat the wrong reasons and perhaps undervalued (and even betrayed) by the very interests he had tried to serve. This work is thus an attempt to appease the ghost of Grierson, if such a thing can be done by someone who, to use Grierson's phrase, is "rotted in the old, untotal ways".[4]

Although others have tried to unravel the Grierson enigma by exploring his realist aesthetic for film or his philosophical eclecticism, I am taking a somewhat different approach. I think one of the keys to understanding Grierson is oil, that black gold which has fuelled so much of this century politically, economically, and socially. As Grierson's biographer Forsyth Hardy indicates, "the biggest volume of sponsorship" for the documentary movement in the 1930s was the oil industry, a connection which continued throughout the war.[5]

Another key to rethinking the Grierson legend is the field of public relations, which was an offspring of monopoly capitalism at the turn of the century and would become central to every aspect of communications and information in the age of mass media. Grierson was one of the first communications specialists to recognize the significant public-relations role that the medium of film might play in a political and corporate context. Although others have implied that the documentary movement was politically hamstrung in its early years by its need for funding and sponsorship from the corporate and government establishment, this text argues that Grierson sought out such sponsorship precisely because he believed in further releasing the potential of the established order.

As film scholar Jack Ellis has observed, during the war Grierson felt that England was missing the "'boundary-crossings in economic terms of world events'. He complained that England looked forward to a post-war world in which things would be back to normal rather than seeing the 'need for new economic integration'."[6] Those economic "boundary-crossings" are an important aspect of Grierson's internationalism. Coupled with his belief in the potential of technology to make both mass production and mass communications more efficient on a global level, Grierson's internationalism was closely aligned with multinational capital's goal to integrate world markets and eliminate the impediments to the new economic order.

Those impediments included organized labour in the form of independent trade unionism; resistance to the ideal of full mechanization and technological progress; and movements towards nationalism and political sovereignty in colonized countries whose resources had long been necessary to U.S. and British corporate expansion. On each of these fronts, Grierson's documentary movement played an important public-relations role. What Eisenstein, Pudovkin, and others had done for the Bolshevik Revolution, what Goebbels would attempt to do for Hitler's National Socialism, Grierson tried to accomplish for multinational capitalism. This thesis is explored from the vantage point of Grierson's war years in Canada, his wartime writings and speeches, and the films made under his tutelage. Of course, such a thesis makes the postwar FBI hounding of Grierson as a "communistic sympathizer" a significant irony in his career, but I attempt to explore other factors involved in this postwar political harassment.

I think Grierson was one of the most brilliant minds of his generation and someone who recognized, as early as the 1920s, something that is only now beginning to be fully understood—that the reproduction of sound and moving image is a far more powerful and psychologically affective medium of communication than print. In an era characterized by ruthlessly competing ideological visions, radio and film were accurately perceived to be the fully mass means through which millions could be mobilized. As an admitted propagandist, Grierson chose the medium of film to serve those aspects of modern society he perceived to be on the side of order, which was his greatest concern.

During the six years of his wartime involvement in Canada, Grierson was in a position of considerable influence and power: drafting Canada's first Film Act; serving as the country's first film commissioner; founding and overseeing virtually every aspect of the new NFB, while simultaneously serving, in 1943 and part of 1944, as the national director of the Wartime Information Board. His official position was just below that of a cabinet minister. Had he not already had easy access to the Prime Minister, his posts would have guaranteed it.

Moreover, he was, by all accounts, a forceful and charismatic personality who ran the newly instituted Film Board with a firm hand. Seemingly authoritarian by nature, Grierson nevertheless expressed throughout his writings and speeches the belief that individualism was a hang-over of nineteenth-century thinking, a hindrance to the whole tenor of this century and to the direction in which he perceived society to be moving. In that sense, this book is less about John Grierson the individual than it is about an era and a way of thinking. That era, and this particular account of it, begin with the turn of the century and with two other figures who were also representative of their times, John D. Rockefeller, Jr., and William Lyon Mackenzie King.

1

Simple Twists of Fate

Something in the nature of continuous administrative machinery for the orderly disposition of controversies is as necessary for the establishment of law and order in Industry as in the State.

WILLIAM LYON MACKENZIE KING

In 1924, 26-year-old John Grierson found himself sailing from his birthplace of Scotland to the United States. After four years of service on a British minesweeper during World War I and another four years at Glasgow University studying moral philosophy, he had been awarded a generous Laura Spellman Rockefeller Memorial fellowship, administered by the Rockefeller Foundation.[1] For the brilliant young Scotsman, it was the chance of a lifetime. The Rockefeller fellowship would pay for his trans-Atlantic fare, his tuition fees at the University of Chicago, his travels around the country, and his living expenses for the duration of his study.[2] As his ship steamed across the Atlantic towards the New World, Grierson must have felt that he was in the hands of destiny. He could not have known, however, that through a simple twist of fate, administered by the Rockefeller Foundation, he was tracing a path that had been travelled ten years earlier by a man who would become his most eminent employer.

In 1914, 40-year-old William Lyon Mackenzie King found himself out of a job. In fact, he'd been out of a job for some time, ever since the Laurier Liberals had been defeated in the general election of 1911 and seven of Laurier's cabinet, including Mackenzie King, had lost their parliamentary seats. Although supported by a generous annuity from one of his many women friends, the ambitious former minister of labour was not at all pleased with his situation. The ironies of it all repeatedly sent him to his diary to pour out his frustrations.

Having spent years as an able civil servant working out the destinies of potential immigrant labourers to Canada, having consulted and conferred with the highest authorities on three continents about "the immigrant problem" and the needs of industry, having himself risen to oversee the Ministry of Labour while some 200 strikes raged across Canada, the former cabinet minister had reached the prime of his life, only to find himself unemployed, out of work, virtually on the dole, had there been a dole in Canada in 1914.

It was unbearable. It was more than humiliating. It deeply offended his sense of destiny. He confided his misery to his diary, how "with the kind of ability I have and the service I might be rendering", his talents were being overlooked. "How terribly broken down on every side is the house of life around me ..."[3].

Many hundreds of miles south of Kingsmere, Ivy Lee in 1914 was finding himself far too much employed. He had known, when oil and mining heir John D. Rockefeller, Jr., had hired him in May, that his public-relations expertise was going to be pushed to the limit. But the incredible pressures of the situation were beginning to hit home. Maybe if he had been hired *before* the massacre, the job of improving the Rockefeller image would have been easier.

In the autumn of 1913, the mine workers in Colorado had reached the limit of their endurance. Mostly immigrant Serbs, Slavs, Welsh, Scots, Italians, and Greeks, they had been encouraged to come to the United States by industrialists in need of a cheap, pliant labour force to work in primary industries—a labour force that would be (or so it was hoped) unorganizable, despite appalling conditions. Labouring 12 hours a day underground, with an average of 100 miners killed every year in industrial accidents, the Colorado mine workers had managed, by 1913, to surpass their polyglot differences and had actively begun to organize, meeting with agents from the United Mine Workers in the hopes of securing better working conditions.

The largest mine operator in the state was Colorado Fuel and Iron Company, which owned 18 mining operations and employed some

12,000 miners and millers in its giant steelworks. Part of the massive Rockefeller holdings, Colorado Fuel ran its operation with an iron fist and no pretence of a velvet glove.

> The miners' low wages (about $1.68 a day) were paid in scrip redeemable only at company stores charging extortionate prices. The miners usually lived in small two-room shacks provided by the company at exorbitant rents, and from which they could be evicted on a three-day notice.... More than $20,000 a year was spent by the company to maintain a force of detectives, mine guards, and spies whose job it was to keep the camps quarantined from the virulence of unionism.[4]

Colorado Fuel adamantly refused to meet with union agents or labour leaders, and in autumn of 1913 the miners finally went out on strike. The company's response was to settle in for a lengthy fight, assisted by its force of private detective agencies skilled in the methods of strike-breaking.

As the strike wore on, Colorado Fuel increased its pressure on the mine workers. During the winter of 1913, 13,000 striking miners and their families were forced out of the company towns to trek down the mountain and seek shelter in tent cities hastily erected by the United Mine Workers. One of the largest of these tent cities was called Ludlow, watched over by a company of paid militia hired by Colorado Fuel. Inevitably, Ludlow was the scene of various bloody provocations throughout the winter. After the strike had lasted seven months, with growing tensions on both sides, the mine owners asked the governor of Colorado to send in the National Guard to keep the situation at Ludlow in check. The governor dutifully complied.

With the National Guard watching over the tent city of increasingly desperate mining families, in April of 1914 Ludlow was a stick of dynamite looking for a match. Just after daybreak on April 20, a shot rang out. The nervous troops opened fire on the city, burning the tents and setting off a pitched battle that raged for days. At the end of the conflagration, nearly 100 miners, women, and children were dead.[5]

The public response to the Ludlow massacre was immediate outrage, with the already unpopular robber-baron Rockefeller family, as the main shareholder and investor in Colorado Fuel and Iron, receiving the brunt of the public's anger. After a month of intense criticism from across the country, Rockefeller Junior sought out Ivy Lee—the noted business consultant who was establishing a new field of public relations to smooth the way for corporate entities in trying times. "I feel," appealed Junior to Ivy Lee, "that my father and I are much misunderstood by the press and the people of this country. I should like to know what your advice would be on how to make our position clear."[6]

After 11 years of working out the bugs in this new field of public opinion, Ivy Lee sensed what needed to be done first. The old way that industrial tycoons and monopoly capitalists had tried to handle controversy—strict silence in the face of a bad press—was, he knew, an outmoded and ineffective tactic. The modern route for those concerned with public opinion was to fight fire with fire, to take the opposition by surprise through a deluge of information stating, in a forthright way, the corporate side of the story. If some business controversy was news, then there was a pressing necessity to help *make* the news, rather than hide behind barriers of silence.

Immediately, Ivy Lee began to issue press releases and news bulletins explaining the events in Colorado. He contacted the network of opinion-makers he had built up over the years—newspaper editors, industrialists, reporters, political friends—and provided them with another angle on the unfolding news story. His press releases and bulletins were later collected in a booklet whose title reveals the particular news slant: *The Struggle in Colorado for Industrial Freedom*.[7]

But even Ivy Lee could see, in May 1914, that a flood of press releases was not going to be enough. With so much public scrutiny focussed on the miners and their situation, with the likes of Upton Sinclair and Carl Sandburg denouncing his employer, with union labour across the country using the situation to expose the workings of monopoly capital in general, a mere outpouring of words from Lee's desk was not the complete answer. Finally he wrote a note to Rockefeller Junior: "It is of the greatest importance that as early as possible some comprehensive plan be devised to provide machinery to redress (the miners') grievances."[8]

But of course, right there was the nub of the problem, as Rockefeller saw it. The United Mine Workers had all along advocated such a plan. This whole intolerable turn of events had developed precisely out of the need to *prevent* the union from redressing grievances. There had to be a way to solve this problem without letting in the likes of John Lawson, Mother Jones, and the other interfering union and labour leaders. There had to be someone in the Western world who could advise him on such things, someone who could deal with these irksome industrial relations and the pressures arising from immigrant labourers and their bleeding-heart sympathizers. There must be someone who could understand the needs of industry, someone who could recognize the role of industry in making the country great. There had to be somebody somewhere who could appreciate that being a millionaire thrust into the glare of the public spotlight was a galling and devilishly delicate situation.

The letter reached William Lyon Mackenzie King in June 1914. Written by Jerome D. Greene, head of the Rockefeller Foundation, it outlined plans for a new department of industrial relations within the foundation, with Mackenzie King serving at its helm. The letter appealed directly and in flattering terms, proposing to Mackenzie King: "You might greatly serve all white race industries and show the way to industrial accord".[9]

Mackenzie King wasted no time thinking about the matter. Here, finally, was a prospect entirely suited to his training, his background, his expertise—which had been languishing unappreciated for so long. In drafting his reply, he recognized that even the outbreak of World War I was fortuitous. Two days after the declaration of war, Mackenzie King furnished his prospective employer with six pages of theory on ways in which the war could prove beneficial to the needs of industrial capitalism, especially through the confusion of organized labour.[10]

Among those presently "embarrassing" the Colorado situation, he wrote, "there are foreigners who may feel compelled to return to Europe." After the hostilities cease, "thousands of men and their families in the Old World are going to seek further employment here in the New. In certain industries it is going to be easy for employers to find all the labor they desire, and unions will be confronted with a new problem."[11] Under the impetus of the new streams of immigration, Mackenzie King argued, the labour unions would "change their policy", putting stress on the necessity of being recognized by companies and using the issue of working conditions to force union recognition.[12] Industries could avoid the whole problem of unions by taking the approach of enlightened self-interest: raising the standards of pay and work on their own initiative.

Such an analysis could not fail to relieve the beleaguered mind of Rockefeller Junior, and after some weeks of negotiating a salary, the formerly unemployed and unappreciated Mackenzie King was offered the position of heading up both a study and a department of industrial relations for the Rockefeller Foundation, at the respectable salary of $12,000 per year.[13] The initial meeting between employer and employee was gratifying on both sides, heralding a lifelong friendship between Rockefeller Junior and Mackenzie King in which "the rapport was permanent; they were to become close as brothers".[14] In October 1914, Mackenzie King formally accepted the post.

The foundation's publicity on the forthcoming labour study emphasized that "in no sense will the investigation be local or restricted, or carried on with particular reference to an existing situation, or for that matter, with reference to conditions in any country ...".[15] But as things turned out, Mackenzie King's attention was primarily focussed on the messy imbroglio at Colorado Fuel and Iron and on the somewhat daunting task confronting Ivy Lee: how to "alter the image of John D. Senior from bloodless robber baron to sweet, harmless, generous old man".[16]

The first necessity was to get a fix on the composition of the labouring masses employed by Colorado Fuel. As Mackenzie King observed:

> It employs between ten and twelve thousand men, pretty evenly divided between the mines and the Steel Mills. The men at both the mines and the mills are of many nationalities. Prior to the War, only 21 per cent. of the employees at the mines were native American [i.e., born in the United States] (14 per cent. white and 7 per cent. colored), 26 per cent. were Italians, 16 per cent. Mexicans, 12 per cent. Austrians, 8 per cent. Greeks, and 16 per cent. a mixture of other nationalities, including English, Scotch, Welsh, Russian, Polish, Roumanian, etc., etc. Of the employees at the mills, a much larger percentage are native Americans.[17]

With the "white race industries" employing such a high percentage of foreign-born workers, the complexities within industrial relations were bound to generate controversy. As Mackenzie King observed in his study, "It is difficult, till a population ceases to be migratory and becomes more or less stationary, to promote industrial development by democratic means."[18] The previous necessity for "autocratic control" by capital and management might now give way to a new attitude in labour relations, or at least one less controversial than before. Mackenzie King set to pondering the situation.

Meanwhile, Ivy Lee was being similarly challenged in his job of image-making. But it was an open field, a pioneering field, and that meant that almost anything could be tried. As one of his public-relations strategies, Lee suggested that Rockefeller Senior walk the streets of New York City giving money away to people. In terms of public opinion, it just might have an affect. The old patriarch must have balked at the suggestion at first. But the dire straits of the family image called for sacrifices on everyone's part. Soon Rockefeller Senior could be seen carrying bags of nickels and dimes to hand out to pedestrians, along with little homilies about the proverbial penny-saved. Simultaneously, Ivy Lee was planting human-interest stories through his newspaper contacts: reported items about Rockefeller's church-going habits, his pleasures in the game of golf, his donations to charity. Newspaper readers at the time also learned of Rockefeller Junior's "spare-time habit of knitting scarves for the doughboys overseas".[19] Not to be outdone by the public-relations brilliance of Ivy Lee, Mackenzie King was offering some useful suggestions of his own.

At Mackenzie King's prompting, Rockefeller Junior invited union organizers and labour leaders to meet with him in his offices, where they could share refreshments and enjoy the affable Rockefeller hospitality, thereby experiencing a more human side of their perceived adversary. According to George McGovern and Leonard Guttridge, authors of *The Great Coalfield War,* this courting of labour leaders "was a successful pioneer essay in public relations and image-making", with even seasoned labour organizers momentarily charmed.[20]

Mackenzie King also helped Rockefeller Junior prepare for his appearances before the goverment's Industrial Relations Commission, which was holding public hearings into the Colorado events. Rockefeller's opening statement was a brilliant gambit, considering the combines investigation of a few years earlier by which the Rockefeller oil trust had been seemingly dissolved into 38 progeny of Standard Oil, but all of them owned by the same group of men and led by Rockefeller himself with a quarter of the shares.[21] Following King's advice, Junior told the commission: "I believe it to be just as proper and advantageous for labor to associate itself into organized groups for the advancement of its legitimate interests as for capital to combine for the same object."[22] Continuing to adhere to Mackenzie King's astute counsel, Rockefeller Junior then "shrugged off question after question with a disclaimer of knowledge, a plea of inadequate background, a regretful admission of no formed opinion. It almost always worked."[23] The Industrial Relations Commission was led to believe that Rockefeller—obviously busy with all the pressing, tycoonish responsibilities of Standard Oil of New Jersey (now Exxon) and other matters—had been uninformed of the situation and the events leading up to the unfortunate disaster at Ludlow, "the most successful police action by federal troops in American labor history".[24]

Then, on September 20, 1915, another of Mackenzie King's useful suggestions fell into place. Rockefeller Junior embarked on a goodwill tour of the 18 Colorado Fuel mining properties, meeting with the miners, sharing lunch with them, swinging a pickaxe in front of the mine face, attending open meetings at their camps—events that generated favourable press copy from the entourage of reporters in attendance. Similarly, Junior's speeches to the miners struck an optimistic note. Mackenzie King, who accompanied his employer on the tour, later wrote:

> To one and all he delivered the same message. "They tell you," he said, referring to popular comment on the disturbances of a few months previous, "that we are enemies. I have come here to tell you that we are not enemies, but partners. Labor and Capital are partners, not enemies. Neither one can get on without the other. Their interests are common, not antagonistic." And so the new policy of Partnership was announced.[25]

To illustrate their common interests, Rockefeller Junior gave a little lesson in economics, explaining that "never since my father and I became interested in this company as stockholders, some fourteen years ago, has there been one cent for the common stock. I just want you to put that in your pipes and smoke it and see if it tallies with what you have heard about the stockholders oppressing you and trying to get the better of you."[26] Obviously, the rich were just as poor as the poor when it came to Colorado Fuel operations. What Junior neglected to mention in his little economics lecture was that the bulk of the Rockefeller equity was in interest-bearing bonds (not stock), which had yielded a return on investment of more than $9 million over the years.[27]

But such tiny discrepancies were to be overlooked in the interest of "common" problems. The partnership of capital and labour became the theme of the tour and the slogan that rippled through the reams of press copy generated by Rockefeller's unprecedented goodwill venture. It was Mackenzie King's answer to the problem of finding a new attitude to replace the old "autocratic control" of industrial management. As the tour moved into its final hours, climaxing with a party for the mine workers, both Mackenzie King and Rockefeller further warmed to the occasion. Whether inspired by his theme of partnership, or moved by the strains of "the Hesitation Waltz" and a bevy of pretty women, Mackenzie King suddenly selected a partner and swirled across the dance floor. Soon Rockefeller himself was dancing with the miners' wives, to the astonishment of all onlookers.[28]

But the highlight of Mackenzie King's work was his solution to the question of a company initiative regarding the grievance process. His Industrial Representation Plan, which he worked out in conjunction with company officials and directors (including Junior), soon became known as the Rockefeller Plan. It provided for the election of two men to represent the miners at each mine, or one for every 150 employees. These elected representatives were to meet annually with an equal number of company officials. The mining camps would be organized into five districts, with meetings scheduled every four months, during which Joint Committees composed of management and labour would discuss health, sanitation, mine safety, recreation, and education.

Periodic tours by a representative of the company president would ensure that harmony was maintained throughout Colorado Fuel's chain of properties. The Plan included clauses forbidding discriminatory practices against workers or job applicants who were past or present members of a union, and for the settlement of grievances, the Plan set up avenues of appeal which reached right to the company president. If necessary, appeals would be taken to the Industrial Commission of Colorado, an institution modelled on one of Mackenzie King's ideas and legislated into existence after the strike.[29]

Mackenzie King saw this as "a wholly new attitude" in industrial relations, a change in policy "from one of exclusive control on the part of Management to one of recognized joint-control on the part of the four parties to Industry: Capital, Management, Labor, and the Community".[30] Compared with Rockefeller Senior's view that paid employment was a charity to workers, Mackenzie King's plan was indeed a step forward.[31] Nevertheless, by establishing management-labour conciliation boards, the Plan effectively reduced the apparent need for unions at all—which was precisely what Colorado Fuel had wanted in the first place when it had refused to meet with union organizers before the strike. The Rockefeller Plan got an immediate reaction from union leaders.

> Organized labor reacted to publicity given the experiment with jeers and skepticism, and it was variously decried as a pseudo-union, a company tool offering workers only the illusion of collective bargaining, a hypocritical pretense of granting what was in reality withheld. It was a device for restoring Rockefeller's reputation and it sapped the spirit of independent labor. It was paternalism's latest and most pernicious guise.[32]

Nevertheless, the Colorado mine workers, worn down on all sides, accepted the Plan, thereby ending the long and bloody dispute.

Rockefeller Junior was unhesitant about expressing his indebtedness to Mackenzie King. "I was merely King's mouthpiece," he admitted. "I needed education. No other man did so much for me. He had vast experience in industrial relations and I had none. I needed guidance. He had an intuitive sense of the right thing to do—whether it was a man who ought to be talked with or a situation that ought to be met."[33] Junior had good reason to be pleased, for what Mackenzie King had done was invent the "company union" which, before it was outlawed in the United States by the Wagner Act of 1935, "was to prove an invaluable instrument for management in blunting the great union drives of the period".[34]

Throughout their lifelong friendship, Rockefeller Junior showed his appreciation to Mackenzie King in a variety of ways, including gifts of $100,000 on two occasions, as well as friendly advice to the lovelorn during Mackenzie King's more romantic years.[35] Strangely enough, Ivy Lee did not fare as well with his employer, though he handled the Rockefellers' publicity for another 15 years. In the 1920s, Standard Oil had entered into a cartel with I.G. Farben, the German petrochemical monopoly, a business relationship that continued during Hitler's rise to power. In 1934, Standard Oil sent Ivy Lee to Germany to consult with Farben and find ways to improve the company's image, as well as that of the Third Reich, to which Farben was closely tied. When Lee returned from Germany, he had to face the Special House Committee on Un-American Activities. As the testimony was released, "the storm of adverse publicity was devastating. Headlines like 'Lee exposed as Hitler Press Agent' broke his spirit and what was left of his health."[36] Under the brunt of intense public criticism, Lee found himself abandoned by the Rockefeller family, which hastened to dissociate itself from such distasteful publicity.[37] Lee died from brain cancer not long after the hearings, thereby ending the whole unsavoury affair.

For his part, Mackenzie King in 1917 was back on track, revitalized. The fortuitous association with Rockefeller Junior and Ivy Lee not only had rescued his flagging career, but also had inspired him with a new vision of international corporate endeavour and the important role of public opinion in the successful management of controversy and labour disputes.

In his text *Industry And Humanity: A Study In The Principles Underlying Industrial Reconstruction* (1918), the work that resulted from his study for the Rockefeller Foundation, he wrote: "Force or Consent: these are the alternative sanctions in all matters pertaining to Law and Government. The democracies of the world have chosen government by

Consent."[38] Within the Colorado Fuel mining imbroglio, he had seen firsthand the disastrous results that had accrued to everyone from the methods of force. And in his clean-up operation for the Rockefeller image, Mackenzie King had also witnessed firsthand the positive results of his, and Ivy Lee's, methods of creating consent. *Industry and Humanity,* besides being an inspired (though unreadable) treatise on the wonders of international capital and world markets, is an extended rumination on the role of public opinion, of the new field of public relations, in the creation of consent. Clearly, government by consent was preferable to government by force, though a third of the way into his text, Mackenzie King let slip this intriguing passage:

> Three or four years ago, I took occasion to inquire of the Royal North-West Mounted Police concerning the methods which have proven so successful in maintaining law and order in unorganized districts of Western and Northern Canada. I was told that the entire districts were regularly patrolled by members of the Force; that settlers were visited upon their farms and ranches, and interviewed concerning violations of the law and the adequacy of the protection afforded.... By this visible link between authority and citizenry, confidence is established and settlement maintained in districts that readily enough lend themselves to depredations and lawlessness.[39]

Apparently, some dialectic between force and consent might be useful, some "visible link between authority and citizenry" to establish "confidence" in all concerned.

Or so the mind of William Lyon Mackenzie King was spinning and speculating as he finished his book and prepared for the 1919 leadership convention of the Liberal Party. He had turned down offers from both the Rockefeller Foundation and the Carnegie Corporation to direct their industrial relations and corporate affairs.[40] Even their offers of an annual income of $30,000 could not tempt him, for William Lyon Mackenzie King had a sense of destiny. As far back as 1901 he had confided to his mother that he would become the prime minister of Canada. In 1919, he could sense that fortune was turning in his favour.

By the time Grierson arrived in the land of opportunity in 1924, the concerns of the Rockefellers had shifted to more in-depth research into U.S. immigration and labour patterns and the necessity for social assimilation into the American melting pot. Though Mackenzie King's work had touched on some of these aspects affecting the operation of "white race industries", his focus had necessarily been the Colorado Fuel and Iron Company. There were, however, bigger patterns in need of examination. John Grierson's proposed subject of study for the Foundation, "Immigration and its effects on the social problems of the United States", held more promise.[41]

After several months of study at the University of Chicago's School of Political Science, Grierson moved to New York City in July 1925. The Rockefeller fellows were encouraged to travel during their studies, and Grierson was eager to do so. His study of immigration and assimilation had quickly led him to recognize that the so-called "yellow press" was, for all its sensationalism, "the most important factor in making over the immigrants from the European way of life to the American way of life".[42] The unquestioned leader in the field was the chain of 18 newspapers owned and overseen by William Randolph Hearst.

Citizen Hearst, the most powerful fabricator of public opinion in the United States, strongly believed that the white race was the only really human race, that the United States would achieve its Manifest Destiny in the world only through a position of strength, and that when it came to identifying the greatest threat to established order, it was a toss-up between communism and the yellow peril.[43] The "pro-fascist" Hearst set the tone for much of popular journalism in the United States from the turn of the century onward.[44] What fascinated Grierson about the Hearst press and its many imitators was the unique style of developing a dramatic story-line to engage the interest of readers.[45] To Grierson, this seemed "a highly logical way of approaching the problem of mass communication".[46] Having recognized the influence of Hearst, Grierson expanded his field of investigation to include "Public opinion–social psychology" and "Newspaper psychology".[47]

In New York, he encountered Walter Lippmann, editor of the *New York World* and author of two seminal texts, *Public Opinion* (1922) and *The Phantom Public* (1925). Clearly in tune with the times, Lippmann recognized the significant role that the mass media were playing in contemporary events through the formation of public opinion. In the intervening years since Ivy Lee and Mackenzie King had explored useful avenues for image-making and the creation of consent, the field of public relations had blossomed. Edward L. Bernays's pioneering handbook, *Crystallizing Public Opinion,* appeared in 1923, providing further convincing testimony (and tactics) for the important role of the new public-relations field.

A brilliant thinker and writer, Lippmann grappled with the democratic implications of the rise of "propaganda by which a private interest seeks to associate itself with the disinterested public".[48] Calling public opinion the "most perplexing" matter in popular government, Lippmann nevertheless espoused the view that Mackenzie King had come to earlier: the larger forces at work in a modern society were beyond the understanding of the average citizen, who could not keep pace with information. There was thus a need for the shaping of public opinion for the masses, for the "manufacture of consent" in Lippmann's phrase, in order to ensure the orderly workings of a complex society. "The public must be put in its place," wrote Lippmann, "so that it may exercise its own powers, but no less and perhaps even more, so that each of us may live free of the trampling and the roar of the bewildered herd."[49] By 1925, Lippmann had come to believe that the role of this "bewildered herd" was to be "interested spectators of action".[50]

> I have, therefore, supposed that the opinions of the spectators must be essentially different from those of the actors, and that the kind of action they were capable of taking was essentially different too. It has seemed to me that the public had a function and must have methods of its own in controversies, qualitatively different from those of the executive men....[51]

Lippmann's views on a society divided into actors and spectators had a lifelong impact on Grierson, whose subsequent career was influenced by this brief encounter.[52] It was Lippmann who encouraged Grierson to turn his attention from newspapers to film in order to explore the more inclusive frame of reference that his research into public opinion and social psychology was leading him to.[53] In their discussion about the "yellow press" and politics, Lippmann accurately recognized that even the Hearst press and its popular influence paled in comparison to Hollywood's extraordinary mass appeal, that, as Grierson recounted it, "'we would do better to follow the dramatic patterns of the film through the changing character of our time, and that the box-office records of success and failure were on file.'"[54] When it came to the "manufacture of consent", there was nothing to equal the power of the movie screen and its story-telling capacities, its ability to address and persuade an audience of millions. By the end of 1925, Grierson was travelling west, meeting with newspaper editors and sitting in on editorial meetings to "observe opinion-forming methods at first hand".[55]

His sights, however, were fixed on that fabled city at the end of the road, Hollywood.

In the early summer of 1926, Grierson reached his destination and began to follow up on Lippmann's advice. Producer Walter Wanger, impressed with the young Grierson, opened up to him the box-office files at Famous Players–Lasky, whose distribution arm was Paramount Pictures, one of the most powerful studio conglomerates in the world.[56] He was soon being paid a retainer by Famous Players–Lasky for analyzing production methods and, in at least one instance, for lecturing at the Paramount Theater Managers Training School on "The Conditions of Popular Appeal", using William Randolph Hearst as the primary model for his analysis.[57] His study for the Rockefeller Foundation became an extended report on the role of cinema, as well as a general report on newspapers, in the formation of public opinion.[58] Thoroughly immersed in the film scene, Grierson began writing film reviews, learning from every source, and formulating his ideas about film as an "easily persuasive" medium.[59]

With his work for the Rockefeller Foundation finished, but with his salary from Paramount Pictures still running, Grierson sailed from New York to London in January 1927.[60] He had read that Great Britain had established the Empire Marketing Board in 1926, an institution intended to "bring the Empire alive in the minds of those who belonged to it and to use every medium of communication to reach the people in the quarter of the world still coloured red on the map".[61] From what he could gather, however, the plan to educate the colonized on the necessities of Empire did not include the use of film. Grierson intended to call upon Stephen Tallents, secretary of the Empire Marketing Board and a pioneer in the field of public relations, to impress upon him the usefulness of film for such a propaganda effort. If society was divided into a "bewildered herd" and an élite of "executive men", leaders of public opinion and a mass of followers, spectators of action and those who act, Grierson knew in 1927 within which category he preferred to be counted.

2

The Age of Consent

This movement [towards corporate concentration] was the origin of the whole system of modern economic administration. It has revolutionized the way of doing business all over the world. The time was ripe for it.... The day of combination is here to stay. Individualism has gone, never to return.

JOHN D. ROCKEFELLER, SR.

Grierson's pitch to Stephen Tallents was forthright. Arguing from what he had learned in his research into film's great mass appeal, he persuaded Tallents that Great Britain's new Empire Marketing Board (EMB) should reconsider the priorities of its media use. Film held great potential for communication, Grierson told Tallents, "but principally there is this thought that a single say-so can be repeated a thousand times a night to a million eyes.... That seven-leagued fact opens a new perspective, a new hope, to public persuasion."[1] Impressed with Grierson's arguments, Tallents hired him to prepare a series of memoranda on the film position of various countries, sending him to France and Germany in 1927.

From the 1890s onwards, American industrialists had focussed their energies not only on amassing vast holdings in a variety of countries and primary industries, but also on achieving vertical integration, the ownership or control of all aspects of a market from production to distribution across the country to ownership of retail outlets. Within the Rockefeller oil empire, for example, Standard Oil pumped and refined the oil and gas, controlled the rails by which it was delivered across the United States, and owned the stations where consumers bought the product.[2]

As a powerful industry in their own right, the Hollywood film studios had early on achieved vertical integration within the United States, producing the films, owning the companies that distributed them, and owning or controlling the theatres where the films were shown. But even more important, the Hollywood conglomerates had become vertically integrated throughout much of the Western world. By the 1920s, Hollywood controlled the screens and box offices of Great Britain, France, Germany, Australia, and Canada, accounting for 90 to 95 per cent of all films shown.[3]

This tight control over the international market meant that countries outside the United States could not build their own film industries. Without access to either distribution or exhibition inside their own borders, foreign film efforts were doomed to failure, at least financially if not artistically. And there was little chance of finding distribution for their films inside the U.S. market. In 1922, for example, "425 foreign films were sent to the U.S. for sale that year, but only 6 were accepted for exhibition."[4] In an attempt to alter their internal situation, certain countries took steps towards protecting their domestic market. Germany, for example, established in the early 1920s a "Kontingent" law, which required that for every foreign (i.e., American) film screened in German theatres a certain number of German films also had to be screened.[5]

By 1922, Hollywood interests had formed a powerful lobby to ensure that such attempts by countries to interfere with American control of the film industry would be effectively curtailed. This lobby, the Motion Picture Association of America (MPAA), quickly formed ties with the U.S. State Department and other governmental sectors to strengthen its effectiveness abroad.

> In 1926, a representative of the American film industry appeared before a committee of Congress to ask for assistance in warding off the threat of foreign legislative enactments aimed at diminishing American influence in the motion picture industry. Congress duly appropriated $15,000 to finance a section of the Department of Commerce to report information regarding such foreign legislation to American producers.[6]

This action was probably the result of legislation passed by Great Britain in 1926, which imposed a stringent quota on American films in order to foster its own indigenous film industry.

In 1927, when John Grierson set out to study the film situation in France and Germany for his report to Stephen Tallents, he was still receiving a salary from Paramount Pictures.[7] This arrangement may well have coloured his perceptions of the film scene in both countries, since Paramount was living up to its name as one of the most powerful worldwide distribution arms operating at the time. With at least some degree of allegiance to Hollywood, and with his own interests crystallizing around the public-relations role of film, Grierson saw no need whatsoever to question the hegemony of the Hollywood structure abroad. Indeed, his report to Tallents advised measures that would leave that structure firmly in place. Since Hollywood's control of film production, distribution, and exhibition was apparently sacrosanct, "There was a case, he argued, for the organization of supplementary production units and supplementary exhibition arrangements ... [in line with] a movement towards special showings by public authorities...."[8] This tactic would leave movie theatres in Hollywood's hands, while attempting to establish a form of non-theatrical distribution and exhibition—an idea Grierson would later have opportunity to develop on an impressive scale.

Having finished his report for Tallents, Grierson began the film-production work that he had urged the EMB to undertake. In 1928, he was appointed chief film officer for the EMB. Relying on established contacts, he wrote to Jesse Lasky at Paramount, suggesting that the U.S. company produce three films for the EMB, all three focussing on Canada, a colony central to not only Great Britain's "quarter of the world still coloured red on the map", but also to Hollywood's extensive empire, which had control of 95 per cent of Canada's box office, with most of that going directly to Paramount Pictures.[9] Meanwhile, Grierson began to gather around him the filmmakers who would become the nucleus of the British documentary movement, including Basil Wright, Paul Rotha, Stuart Legg, Arthur Elton, John Taylor, Edgar Anstey, and Harry Watt.

The bulk of the film output by the EMB in the years 1928-33 is, according to Elizabeth Sussex, "of mainly academic interest today", with only two films, *Drifters* and *Industrial Britain,* standing out as major accomplishments.[10] Nevertheless, this early period of Grierson's film career reveals interesting aspects of his thinking. Several of the films involved joint-sponsorship with corporate industry. For example, both *Cargo from Jamaica* and *Windmill in Barbados* were financed by the EMB and the Orient Shipping Line, while *Voice of the Wind,* a film about developments in the medium of radio, was partially sponsored by a gramophone company, His Master's Voice.[11] According to Paul Rotha, many of the films were intended "to advertise the natural wealth of the Empire", serving as "predecessors of the TV commercial" in their public-relations function.[12]

Within that function, there was a need to delineate two important aspects: the "necessity" of the colonial structure and the place of labour. As media scholar Stuart Hood has noted, the EMB films made under Grierson's leadership were strongly imperialist in their assumptions, rarely questioning the exploitation of colonial labour and the colonies themselves.[13] As virtual public-relations films for the British Empire, the EMB output expressed privileged and élitist assumptions about the righteousness of colonial domination.[14]

But such an attitude could not be stated so forthrightly. In 1933, Grierson looked back on his six years with the EMB and summarized the thrust of his endeavour:

> Its principal effect ... was to change the connotation of the word 'Empire'. Our original command of peoples was becoming slowly a co-operative effort in the tilling of soil, the reaping of harvests, and the organization of a world economy. For the old flags of exploitation it substituted the new flags of common labour; for the old frontiers of conquest it substituted the new frontiers of research and world-wide organization.[15]

Grierson's language and rhetoric here are characteristically ambiguous. As a propagandist, he was learning the usefulness of the ambivalent phrase embedded within a thicket of clichés. He does not state what is meant by "a world economy" or "the new frontiers of research and world-wide organization". Phrases like "co-operative effort" and "new flags of common labour" sound vaguely appealing and fall well within the discourse of consent, replacing the old words associated with force, such as "command", "exploitation", and "conquest". Nevertheless, such phrases hide their meaning.

For example, "co-operative effort in the tilling of soil" suggests co-operatives, or co-operation. But in 1932, a year before he wrote this, Grierson used the word "co-operative" to convey a quite different attitude and meaning. He wrote of "the essentially co-operative or *mass nature* of society".[16] Thus, his reference in 1933 to "co-operative effort" is actually to mass labour, mass work.

With the workforce defined in terms of its mass nature, the meaning of Grierson's reference to "the new frontiers of research and world-wide organization" becomes somewhat clearer. Industry at the time was steeped in Taylorism and assembly-line techniques, time-motion studies, efficiencies of mass production, and the organization of mass labour for such production. During the 1920s, the industrial engineer Charles Bedaux began making his millions by advising companies, such as ITT, Standard Oil, General Motors, and Ford, on ways to streamline production through assembly-line speedups and reorganizing plants on the basis of time-motion efficiencies.[17] Grierson's interest in such technological rationalization of the production process is hinted at in the changed connotation for the word "Empire", which he claimed EMB had accomplished. What the EMB had done, he recalled in 1937, was "to bring the Empire alive in contemporary terms, as a commonwealth of nations and as an international combine of industrial, commercial, and scientific forces".[18] Within those forces, the place of mass labour needed articulation. To that end, the role of propagandist cinema was to be, according to Grierson, "a documentary of industrial and social function".[19]

Basil Wright, who had been sent by the EMB and Orient Shipping Line to the West Indies to film material for *Cargo from Jamaica* and *Windmill in Barbados,* related this anecdote:

> I'd got this material which I knew was going to lead up to this appalling scene on the dockside, with all these men being paid about a farthing a day for doing this tremendously hard work. I filmed it from every possible dynamic angle, because my desire was to show the toil and sweat involved in this particular work [loading banana boats]—and, indeed, the exploitation.[20]

According to Wright, Grierson told him "You can have your violence" but recommended that he incorporate some footage that Grierson had shot, placing it at the end of the film. "He'd done some of these very calm shots of the bananas in London coming along these endless belts with nobody touching them, nobody doing any hard work at all."[21] Grierson felt that such an ending would make a "lovely contrast".[22] It was as well a scene that highlighted the benefits of technological mass production suited to the "international combine of industrial, commercial, and scientific forces" that Grierson admired.

Ironically, Grierson's work for the EMB from 1928 to 1933 earned the Film Unit the label of "going Bolshevik". One reason for the charge was the importance that Grierson and his filmmaking colleagues attached to the contemporary work of Russian filmmakers like Pudovkin and Eisenstein.[23] But if admiration of Russian filmmaking was a sign of Bolshevism, then Joseph Goebbels himself was a Bolshevik, since he had long considered Eisenstein the leader in cinematic technique. By March 1933 Hitler's newly appointed Minister of Popular Enlightenment and Propaganda was suggesting that Eisenstein's *Battleship Potemkin* be the model for Nazi cinema.[24] Goebbels's frequent, flattering references to Eisenstein's film work finally prompted the Soviet filmmaker to publish an open letter to Goebbels in 1934, denouncing the Nazi propagandist and everything he stood for.[25]

The EMB unit also earned the "going Bolshevik" label because the films incorporated images of working people. As Grierson recalled in 1937, "The thought of making work an honoured theme, and a workman, of whatever kind, an honourable figure, is still liable to the charge of subversion."[26] Although in some ways it was an innovation in Britain at the time to depict the worker on the screen, there is a certain irony in the EMB being labelled Bolshevik for doing so. As Elizabeth Sussex notes, "the fishermen in *Drifters* and the various craftsmen in *Industrial Britain* are shown from what would today be regarded as a middle-class, establishment viewpoint":

> The attitude in the films is that work is in itself ennobling, and hence it is no part of the general purpose to get too close to working people as people, to reveal their pay or their living conditions, the price paid to them or the price they paid.[27]

Sussex claims, however, that despite the middle-class perspective of the films, "it was obviously progressive to show working people at all."[28] This is a questionable claim in the light of Stuart Hood's observation that "the concept of the dignity of labour" is "a concept which can be adapted to fit into the most reactionary of political philosophies (Fascism, for instance), but which was to become an important element in the work of the British documentary group."[29] Although previous mainstream film depictions of labour had shown workers as comic buffoons or background servants, the documentary movement spearheaded by Grierson championed the dignity of work but largely "avoided crucial questions about wages and conditions".[30]

I think that what Grierson brilliantly recognized at the time was that, in the midst of significant challenges to modern capitalism brought on by both the Soviet revolution and the stock market crash, there was a need to portray the working class, and colonized labour, in ways that would maintain the status quo. To leave labour undepicted on film would be to ignore a significant sector whose consent was necessary to the unfolding of capitalism's next stage. As well, to overlook the depiction of labour on film by mainstream interests would simply be handing over that depiction to the more radical elements of society, to those inspired by the Soviets and their brilliant use of cinema. Thus, documentary film under Grierson's leadership had a public-relations role to play in the prevention of radical change and in the "manufacture of consent" to the powers of the status quo.

As Stuart Legg candidly recalled in his 1970s interview with Elizabeth Sussex:

> In the early thirties you had in this country [Great Britain] what was virtually a pre-revolutionary situation, owing to the Depression. There was a need on the part of governments for communication, and a little later, industries too.... Now it is possible, I think, to accuse the documentary movement of, in principal [sic] at least, being prepared to sell itself to the wishes of the government, of the major industries, the Establishment, the capitalists, whatever you like.[31]

Legg attributes this sellout to "the sponsorship formula ... devised by Grierson".[32]

In 1942, Grierson looked back on the work of the British documentary movement of the 1930s and summarized its effort:

> We were concerned not with the category of 'purposiveness without purpose' but with that other category beyond which used to be called teleological. We were reformers, open and avowed: concerned—to use the old jargon—with 'bringing alive the new materials of citizenship', 'crystallizing sentiments' and creating those 'new loyalties from which a progressive civic will might derive'. Take that away and I'd be hard put to say what I have been working for these past fifteen years.[33]

It is important to note that this reformist effort was devoted to changing the attitudes of the viewing public and working people, not to reforming any of those industrial, commercial, and scientific forces that were reshaping the world. That "international combine" of forces was apparently sacrosanct, if in need of "new loyalties" from the public. Thus, the word "progressive" as used by Grierson did not necessarily imply social and political reform based on principles of equality or redistribution of society's resources and wealth. Collier and Horowitz write of there being, during the 1930s, certain "'progressive' trends" that were transforming the industrialized world: the "centralization of administrative units, the growth of scientific ideas and technology, and the internationalization of American influence and power".[34] Such "progressive" trends were part of Rockefeller Junior's vision for the future, and that of other corporate industrialists during the Depression. These tenets of modernism had been formulating since the turn of the century, but during the early 1930s, with the status quo rocked to its foundation, the need for such efficiency, control, and multinational expansion had become clearly evident. While maintaining contact with the Rockefeller Foundation throughout the 1930s, Grierson was also further refining his ideas about the role of documentary cinema in attaining the goal of internationalization.[35]

In the middle of his work for the EMB, Grierson was sent by Stephen Tallents on another fact-finding tour, this time to Canada in 1931, a trip that followed close on the heels of the passage of the Statute of Westminster by which Canada as a Dominion achieved constitutional equality within the Commonwealth of the United Kingdom. Grierson's assignment was "to report on the strength of the nationalistic spirit in Canada and especially the strength of the English spirit in Toronto".[36] The needs of the British Empire were not particularly well served by any movement towards Canadian nationalism; whatever use Tallents was making of Grierson's findings, they focussed (according to Grierson biographer Forsyth Hardy) on two main concerns.

First, Grierson discovered that the colony was proving itself competitive in the area of government-sponsored film. The Canadian Government Motion Picture Bureau, a branch of the Department of Trade and Commerce, not only had excellent film equipment but was also reaching an audience of some 25 million in North America each year.[37] Grierson reported to Tallents that, although the films themselves left something to be desired, there was little doubt that Frank Badgley's bureau "made our Unit [the EMB] seem a very poor relation indeed.... In cinema qualities we have not so much to learn on this side, but on the equipment side and in the creation and management of circulation [film distribution] we have almost everything [to learn]."[38]

Second, Grierson studied the degree of assimilation of immigrant groups into the dominant Anglo-colonial fabric of Canada, an issue apparently of interest to Tallents. Against the background of his study for the Rockefeller Foundation, Grierson "noted that the melting-pot process in the United States had not been repeated in Canada, largely because the French-Canadian initiative in maintaining an ethnic cultural identity had encouraged the other groups—Ukrainians, Italians, Greeks, Scots—to retain theirs also."[39] Canadian nationalism, Canadian government filmmaking, and the multicultural fabric of Canadian society were issues that grew in importance to the centre of Empire as it moved inexorably towards war. Meanwhile, Grierson met with various Canadian parliamentary ministers, newspaper editors, opinion-makers, and the president of the National Research Council to discuss possible subjects for films from the EMB.[40]

After the EMB was disbanded in 1933, Grierson turned his producer talents to the formation of a film unit for the General Post Office (GPO), while also seeking corporate sponsorship for other film projects. The political effect of patronage has been noted in some of the more celebrated films of this period. For example, *Song of Ceylon* was a beautiful, award-winning film, but as Stuart Hood observes, "it totally avoids the question of colonial labour and the economic exploitation of the colonies—which is not surprising, since it was produced by the GPO Film Unit in conjunction with the Ceylon Tea Propaganda Board."[41]

Other films revealed a technological fetish developing in the documentary movement. As Paul Rotha complained, "although Grierson's films were very good technically, 'the people in them were mostly the men behind the machines; you knew nothing about them.' The hero of *Night Mail* 'is the train, not the people on the train'."[42] Nonetheless, the success of the films increased the stature of Grierson's film unit and led to interest from other sectors. As Stuart Legg recalled, "when the GPO began to get a reputation, industry got interested in the use of this new medium of public relations."[43]

The "first and greatest of the sponsors", to use Grierson's own words, was Shell Oil, which "saw the full implications of its international operation".[44] The Shell Film Unit was formed in 1934, based on a report written by Grierson for Shell International. The report was instigated by Jack Beddington, director of publicity for Shell–Mex BP.[45] Grierson's consulting advice on the public-relations use of film by Shell led to an important association with Beddington and Shell–Mex BP which lasted through the war. The implications of this association reveal themselves in the messy politics of oil as they were being played out on the world scene at the time.

By the 1920s, the three world leaders in the oil industry were the Rockefellers' Standard Oil, whose president, Walter Teagle, presided over all aspects of the business; Royal Dutch Shell, an international conglomerate run by Henri Deterding; and British Petroleum (BP), overseen by Sir John Cadman (with Winston Churchill, who had bought up half the company in 1914, operating behind the scenes).[46] The Big Three had effectively divided up the world's oil reserves into various corporate spheres of interest, although that did not stop them from engaging in fierce competition among themselves. In their search for oil reserves, the greatest fear shared by the Big Three was the spectre of countries nationalizing their oil, as the Bolsheviks had done in the Soviet Union after 1917.[47] In that instance, Standard Oil had suffered badly from the Communists' expropriation of the country's oil fields, which were producing 15 per cent of the world's oil at the time. Rubbing salt into the wound, the Soviets then offered their oil at cut prices to Standard's competitors, including Shell and BP which were trying to make deals with the Soviets.[48]

The spectre of nationalization was particularly feared by the British Empire, which had no oil reserves of its own until the discovery of oil in Burma. Through the 1920s, BP "was resented by foreign countries, particularly colonial countries, as an arm of the government".[49] Standard Oil, Shell, and BP obviously preferred to see oil-producing countries follow the model of Venezuela, whose dictator, Juan Vincente Gomez, had since 1908 liberally distributed his country's oil gushers to all comers, especially Gulf, Standard Oil, and Shell.[50] But the Venezuela model was not universally adopted, and the Big Three were forced to continue their political interventions and their fierce competition. This did not stop them, however, from also making deals and solidifying expedient, if temporary, friendships among themselves. In 1928, Teagle of Standard Oil, Cadman of BP, and Deterding of Shell began to hold secret conferences to try to limit their destructive competition.[51] The underlying message of this international cartel, formed to control production and prices among themselves and smaller companies, was that Standard Oil could no longer hope to achieve a global monopoly and would instead have to deal with Shell and BP as equals.[52]

Soon, the potential spin-offs of such corporate co-operation were made evident. In 1930, Argentine president Hipolito Yrigoyen "sealed his own fate" when he refused to hand over Argentine oil to Standard and Shell and was instead interested in doing business with the Soviets.[53] He was overthrown by a military coup engineered by capitalist interests, ushering in the era of military dictatorship in Argentina. But other situations brought out that old competitive urge between companies. In 1932, Bolivia and Paraguay, the two poorest countries in

South America, went to war. "Concealed in the folds of both flags, Standard Oil and Royal Dutch Shell [were] disputing the oil of the Chaco", a bit of map bordering both countries.[54] While warring on the Chaco, however, there was one thing on which both Teagle and Deterding did agree: the necessity for the "capitalist domination of Europe and the ultimate need to destroy Russia".[55]

By the early 1930s the Big Three were meeting to ensure that no company undercut another and that, through local allies, deals could be made in individual countries. "One of the most effective was Britain, where Shell and BP collaborated with Exxon to fix prices, and also formed a joint British marketing company called Shell–Mex BP (which remained together into the mid-seventies, when it was dissolved after long and painful negotiations)."[56] As of 1933, at least two members of Shell–Mex BP—Deterding's Shell and Teagle's Standard Oil—had made deals with Hitler's finance minister in support of the Third Reich.[57] The appeal of the new Hitler regime to Standard Oil and Shell may have been based on Hitler's explicit hatred of Bolshevism, his plan to crush the Soviet Union, to drive trade unionism out of Germany, and to return business to its rightful position as "masters in their own house".[58]

By the time Grierson was advising Shell International on its public-relations use of film in 1934, Deterding had become adamantly pro-Nazi; he was "convinced that the Nazis were the only solution to the Communist menace".[59] Remaining in his post as director general of Shell until sometime after 1936, Deterding was finally eased out by his fellow directors and went to live on his estate in Germany, where he continued to be staunchly anti-communist until his death just before the outbreak of war.[60]

Given such a politically right-wing background to one of the documentary movement's major sponsors, Grierson's later explanation of Shell's sponsorship seems somewhat understated:

> Shell Oil was the first and greatest of the sponsors because it saw the full implications of its international operation, its full implication in terms of instruction, in terms of social welfare and the preaching and teaching of social welfare. For example, one of the propositions that was first put to us in the early thirties was that they found in the Gulf of Persia that it took two men to lift a bag of cement. Therefore, they were in the nutrition business. So they were in the business not only of creating a new nutritional basis but of teaching nutrition, teaching sanitation, and so on.

> Well, they worked logically into all kinds of services of an educational or inspirational kind in the communities in which they operated, whether it was in Venezuela, whether it was in the Upper Persian Gulf, or whether it was in the Dutch East Indies.[61]

Indicating that Grierson was unable or unwilling to alter his attitudes towards colonialism, his statement also hints at his view of multinationals: that, through enlightened self-interest, they might actually benefit the colonized. Stuart Hood, while noting that Shell's "nutrition business" was devoted to "seeing that each man could carry his own bag and thus increase productivity and Shell's profits", nevertheless considers Grierson's approach to have been "purely pragmatic".[62] But pragmatic in service to what interests?

Grierson's association with Shell–Mex BP in the early 1930s seems to have provided him with a model for his political vision. As a price-fixing organization and joint marketing company for the Big Three, Shell–Mex BP was the first tangible and pragmatic instance of competitors merging their interests for harmonious co-operation. Beddington's Shell–Mex BP was an illustration of the "progressive" argument being advanced in the early 1930s in favour of multinational corporations: "that they serve as buffers to soften confrontations between states, whereas national companies exacerbate the conflicts".[63]

Not surprisingly, then, the British documentary movement of the 1930s saw itself in competition with, and inevitably superior to, other more radical film movements in Britain at the time, such as the Workers' Film and Photo League, Kino, Atlas, and People's Newsreel.[64] Their makeshift production conditions and low budgets were in stark contrast to Grierson's methods and funding, as his documentarians lined up sponsored film work for Shell, BP, Imperial Chemical Industries, British Commercial Gas Association, Imperial Airways, London Transport, and a number of other industrial groups. According to Elizabeth Sussex, "Finance for documentary with a social purpose was to come largely from industry. *Housing Problems* [made for the gas industry] had demonstrated that an industrial sponsor, unlike the government, might enhance its own image by exposing bad social conditions."[65]

By 1936, the documentary movement was attracting widespread attention, especially from various film societies, which recognized the aesthetic qualities of much of the work. Although Grierson himself was somewhat dismissive of these "circles devoted to the art of cinema", noting that they "mean well" but have "a certain shallowness of outlook" which missed the propagandistic intent of the material, he was not about to turn away interest from any sector.[66]

The international use of film was perceived to fit well within the "progressive" agenda of the emergent multinationals, and through the 1930s both the Carnegie Corporation, the philanthropical arm of Carnegie's United States Steel Corporation, and the Rockefeller Foundation provided funding for various film society movements, including the National Film Society of Canada, founded in the mid-1930s.[67] Under the leadership of Donald Buchanan, the National Film Society moved quickly to ease the customs regulations covering entry of foreign films into Canada for educational purposes. Ross McLean, who had helped Buchanan with the founding of the film society, had moved on to become secretary to Vincent Massey, Canada's high commissioner in London. McLean continued to be passionately interested in films and, at Massey's request, began a study of the British documentary movement. After meeting Grierson, McLean sent a favourable report to Massey, expressing his interest in having Grierson take a hand in developing Canadian film. Massey forwarded the report to Prime Minister Mackenzie King in 1936.[68]

While the inevitable bureaucratic delays postponed a response from the Canadian government, Grierson left the film unit of the General Post Office and moved on to more corporate concerns. There were evident limitations to what state sponsorship of film might achieve, especially with regard to "Grierson's dream to lift documentary film out of the national and into the international context".[69] Though Shell International had quickly recognized the usefulness of documentary in shaping public opinion, other corporate bodies had been somewhat slower to see the importance of film in the age of consent. Grierson's view on corporate sponsorship of documentary films included the belief that private enterprise "should prove that its private opportunity was a public responsibility", and that, in their own interest, private corporations "must relate to the people's needs and, therefore, to their imagination".[70] Grierson hoped that the example of non-government sponsorship of films would spread abroad, especially to the United States, where such an approach to the "manufacture of consent" could prove useful, given the difficulties of the Depression years.[71]

In 1937, Grierson decided to establish an independent Film Centre to make films sponsored by the private sector. With filmmakers Stuart

Legg and Arthur Elton and administrator J.P.R. Golightly, the Film Centre "set the precedent for public relations films" in its subsequent work.[72] From its beginning, Grierson's Film Centre had a formal link with Shell–Mex BP, which persisted throughout the war years, and with Shell International until well into the postwar era.[73]

Grierson also maintained his contacts with Sir Stephen Tallents, who by 1937 had moved on to administer the Imperial Relations Trust, a shadow organization possibly connected to Britain's secret service and concerned with British propaganda efforts for the war looming on the horizon.[74] As film advisor to the Trust, Grierson was commissioned in 1938 to travel to Canada, New Zealand, and Australia to survey the possibilities of setting up a film centre in each of these countries with a view towards "strengthening the link between Britain and the dominions if war came".[75] There was a growing need for improved communication between the Empire and its far-flung periphery, and film had obviously proven itself to be a powerful propaganda tool. More significantly, Grierson's assignment for the Imperial Relations Trust included a specific goal. As Gary Evans has revealed, that goal was "to set up a North American propaganda base to urge Canada and (more important) the United States into an active partnership with Britain at war, if war should come".[76]

Through a simple twist of fate, this assignment neatly coincided with the long-delayed invitation from the Canadian government asking Grierson to come to Canada and survey the film situation.[77] So, in 1938, under hire to the Imperial Relations Trust and simultaneously hosted by a willing Canadian government, Grierson set out to survey the potential of film production in Canada.

In his third term as prime minister, William Lyon Mackenzie King had more than fulfilled his early promise to his mother, but in 1938 much remained to be done. Returning again and again to the prescient wisdom expressed in his *Industry and Humanity*, a work from which he quoted throughout his lifetime,[78] Mackenzie King may have noted the contemporary relevance of his prophetic statement about the need for "something in the nature of continuous administrative machinery for the orderly disposition of controversies".[79] Perhaps film could fulfil such a need. In any case, this John Grierson from England spoke in glowing terms of the persuasive power of the medium. Here was someone who recognized the necessity of consent within a democracy, who understood public opinion, who even had a background similar to his own in important respects: the work for the Rockefeller Foundation, the study of immigration and labour problems, the research into the whole field of public opinion and its significance to modern times. There was much in common between the two men. According to Forsyth Hardy, "the relationship became 'What Grierson says goes.'"[80]

3

Spectacle, Absences, and the Economy of God

Each nation may yet find the salvation of its own industrial life by losing itself in an effort to save the industrial lives of other and rival nations. It is in such ways, through the course of time, that the economy of God gains world expression.

WILLIAM LYON MACKENZIE KING

In 1938, Grierson travelled across Canada, meeting with Prime Minister Mackenzie King and Tory leader R.B. Bennett, several ministers of Parliament, as well as with newspaper editors and civic leaders in major cities. On one point, they were all agreed: film "should be used to diminish sectionalism and give Canada a sense of its relationships at home and overseas".[1] As Grierson reported to the Imperial Relations Trust, "In most discussions, I presented the notion that the most important federal media were those which imaginatively brought alive one part of the country to another, and dramatised relationships as distinct from differences...."[2]

That variety of ethnic and cultural identities, which Grierson had noted in his 1931 tour of Canada, had also been of increasing concern to politicians and business leaders. John Herd Thompson notes in *Canada 1922-1939: Decades of Discord* that "by 1931 these 'foreigners' comprised one fifth of the labour force in manufacturing, and a wide swath of the rural population in the Prairie Provinces".[3] As the Dirty Thirties got underway with a vengeance, perceived threats to the established order mounted. Elected in 1930, Bennett's Conservative government adopted a policy of summarily deporting immigrants who engaged in "radical activities", ridding the country of more than 10,000 people between 1931 and 1934.[4] When Canadians by the thousands submitted petitions of protest, Justice Minister Hugh Guthrie stated in the House of Commons in 1933:

> I have now ceased to acknowledge receipt of them [the petitions]. I merely hand them over to the mounted police in order that a record may be kept of the names and addresses. I can assure the House that ... there does not appear a single Anglo-Saxon or French-Canadian name—nothing but the names of foreigners, unpronounceable names for the most part.[5]

Although it is not true that the petitioners were mainly "foreigners", the powers of state were primarily afraid of potential "ethnic radicals" within the Ukrainian, Hungarian, Czech, Jewish, and other communities in Canada.[6] By 1938, all the opinion-makers across the country confirmed to Grierson the pressing need to "diminish sectionalism".

Grierson completed his "Report on Canadian Government Film Activities" in August of 1938 and returned to England, where he prepared an abridged edition of the report for the Imperial Relations Trust.[7] According to Forsyth Hardy, Grierson "found three main weaknesses in Canada: lack of a considered directive for Canada as a whole; lack of a strong creative film unit to carry out the policy and interpret it in imaginative terms; and the parochialism of the different departments".[8] He recommended "a continuing committee to keep Canadian propaganda film policy under review", a strengthening of the role of the government film officer, and "that the Motion Picture Bureau should be given creative manpower".[9]

The report was favourably received by the Mackenzie King government, and in November of 1938, Grierson returned to Canada to draft the legislative bill to create a national film board, with the help of J.F. McNeil of the Department of Justice.[10] The bill included the appointment of a film commissioner for a three-year term to oversee the production and distribution of films. By the time the bill was introduced in the House of Commons in March 1939, Grierson had returned to Great Britain.

Responsible for the legislative bill was Minister of Trade and Commerce W.D. Euler. He argued persuasively during the House of Commons debate:

> It must be evident that film has advanced to the stage where it may often be in the national interest to prepare films which will serve national

> purposes as distinct from those of any individual [government] department.... That is the real purpose. There is, however, a more or less remote object, and that is the getting out of what may be called national film ... the distribution of national films designed to help Canadians in all parts of Canada to understand the ways of living and problems of Canadian people.[11]

While the House was debating the merits of the National Film Act, finally giving it royal assent in May, Grierson embarked on travels connected with his Film Centre in London and his assignment for the Imperial Relations Trust. From the United States, he wrote to Stephen Tallents expressing his concern about the ineffectiveness of British propaganda there. "It cannot be sufficiently emphasised", he wrote, "that we have not yet got hold of American opinion. The isolation sentiment is strong and minds are doubtful of the rights and wrongs of the European issue."[12] Meanwhile, the Mackenzie King ship of state embarked on its own public-relations attempts to diminish sectionalism and create unity. The Bennett government's tactics of force had obviously not proved entirely effective. Mackenzie King, on the other hand, had an intuitive and experiential grasp of that modernist project: the manufacture of consent.

In terms of spectacle, 1939 was a banner year for Canada. Across North America, movie fans were flocking to see Shirley Temple, Randolph Scott, and Margaret Lockwood in *Susannah of the Mounties* (from Twentieth Century–Fox), Charles Starrett in *Outpost of the Mounties* and *North of the Yukon* (from Columbia Pictures), and that celebrated series from Monogram Pictures, *Renfrew of the Mounted,* starring James Newill. Not to be outdone by Hollywood, the Canadian apparatus of state had arranged its own awesome series of spectacle.

In mid-May 1939, Canada played host to King George VI and Queen Elizabeth. Travelling in their elaborately appointed silver and blue Royal Train, the British monarchy, with Mackenzie King in attendance, neatly encircled the territory of the Dominion on the nation-building tracks of the Canadian National Railway. A lavish public-relations tour timed to crystallize colonial sentiment and ties to an England on the edge of war, the month-long Royal Visit nevertheless incorporated its own seeming contradiction.

Three weeks into the tour, Queen Elizabeth was asked to officially dedicate the new super-highway being constructed in southern Ontario and named in her honour, the Queen Elizabeth Way (QEW). The first superhighway on the North American continent—with advanced cloverleaf construction, divided lanes, and incandescent and sodium-vapour lighting along lengthy portions of its four-lane route—the QEW was being constructed to provide a more efficient transportation link between Ontario and the United States.[13] In the language of the hype used to herald this new era of international transportation, the QEW would provide for the United States "an open door to Canada and its great resources".[14] Assumed to be a door that would primarily open inward, providing easy access to central Canada's territorial space and resource wealth, the QEW was being hastened towards completion with all the urgency that Canada's state apparatus could muster.

History does not record whether or not Her Majesty balked at, or even recognized, the ironies involved in officiating over the dedication of this new north-south axis named in her honour. Perhaps she, too, was dazzled by these four lanes of smooth pavement stretching between Toronto and the U.S. highway system—a system obviously being trumped and surpassed by this colossal effort on the part of the Canadian state. Whatever the case, the Queen's official ride along the QEW on June 7, 1939, seems a particularly resonant moment in Canada's prewar history.

On the one hand, the Royal Tour crossing the country via nineteenth-century rail technology graphically underlined the enduring claims of the Old World Empire. As the Royal Train sped across the Canadian landscape, its path inscribed a "Canada" defined by England, whose imperialist interests in the Dominion had not abated, though its financial investment and holdings in the country had steadily decreased. On the other hand, the Queen's blessing of a new transport technology and a new vertical axis signified the importance of the tie forged between New World neighbours through an "open door" leading north. Although Great Britain's investment in Canada had shrunk appreciably between 1913 and 1939 (from $2.818 to $2.476 billion), U.S. investment and holdings had risen by a factor of five during the same period (from $835 million to $4.151 billion)—an extraordinary expansion based on the growth of U.S. branch plants in Canada from the 1920s onward.[15] The construction of the QEW, begun in 1931 and hastened as the decade approached its end, thus inscribed a "Canada" defined in terms of the United States, the emerging New World Empire.

The Queen's royal ride along the QEW thereby underscored, for all concerned, the intended role and place of Canada in forthcoming events. The prospect of war on the horizon called forth the necessity of articulating, even symbolically, the interrelationships among allies. Defined in terms of both the Old and the New World Empire, Canada could and would accommodate each one. And as a north-south axis, the QEW was symbolically a bridge—as Canada itself was to be—between Great Britain and its former colony. As the Queen's limousine sped south along the QEW in the dedication ceremony, its path symbolically traced the mediating role that Canada would play between the two world powers. (Perhaps appropriately for Mackenzie King's vision for his country, the QEW had previously been known as "the Middle Road" before its name was switched to generate private capital.)

At the same time these paths were being inscribed upon Canadian ground in 1939, and with all the hoopla that Canadian political and business leaders could generate, there was another route whose construction was being decisively postponed. The urgency given to the completion of the four-lane, divided, clover-leafed, sodium-vapour lit, paved QEW superhighway meant that plans for the construction of the Trans-Canada Highway—an east-west link across the provinces—were placed in limbo, with the existing road remaining an uncompleted, two-lane, gravelled route until long after the war. Both the Ontario government of Mitch Hepburn and the federal government of Mackenzie King gave highest priority to the QEW and refused to spend money completing even the gaps in the rough trans-Canada road. As historian Robert M. Stamp ironically observes, "Four lanes of pavement between Toronto and the United States were much more important than two lanes of gravel between Toronto and Winnipeg."[16]

The completion of the Trans-Canada Highway would have meant that internal and interprovincial relations and business within a vast and diversely populated country were being consciously forged and preferred over north-south interests. Between 1931 and 1939, Ontario alone invested some $550 million in the QEW.[17] Had that money been put into the proposed Trans-Canada Highway, the resulting message from Central Canada to the other provinces, as well as from the Canadian state to the United States, would have been decisively different. Defining Canada in terms of its own provinces, this alternative route posed an "open door" east and west, providing ease of interprovincial access and a modernized link from coast to coast. This proposed Trans-Canada Highway potentially signified a different ideological path for the country in the 1930s. Its very absence resonated behind the state-arranged moments of spectacle mounted in 1939.

At virtually the same time that the Royal Visit and the QEW were converging in the Queen's royal ride, another extraordinary public-relations event was unfolding. The New York World's Fair opened to massive international crowds. Centred around the theme, "The World of Tomorrow", the fair provided a vivid forum in which participating nations could display their own visions of themselves in a hoped-for future. Along with 60 other countries, Canada provided a portrait of its future self in the Canada Pavilion, whose interior display was supervised by W.D. Euler, minister of trade and commerce.

The spectacular centrepiece of the Canada Pavilion was a huge copper map of the country covering an area of 1,000 square feet. Upon this gleaming metallic surface were illuminated various points of interest, as determined by the Department of Trade and Commerce. These included cities, industrial centres, national playgrounds, harbours, transportation routes, water-power resources, significant mineral deposits, wheat-growing districts, and RCMP outposts.[18] On either side of this map were two huge murals, one entitled "Canada at Play" and the other "Canada at Work". The first depicted various scenic vacation spots across the country in a seemingly unpopulated vista of natural wonders and tourist hotels; the second depicted a massive hydro-electric power plant providing energy to a variety of industries. Similar to the "At Play" mural in its unpeopled abstraction, the "At Work" mural highlighted the prospect of a massive technological dynamo keeping the engines of industry moving.

Significantly, the titles of these murals refer not to Canadians but to Canada, and the scenes show, not people at play and at work, but a country that is temptingly displaying itself, boosting its playgrounds, its natural resources, its potential for industrial development, its empty space ripe for exploitation.

The underlying message of all this was not lost on Canadian visitors to the fair. Many found the Canada Pavilion "a scene of humiliation".[19] One reviewer names the problematic oversight perpetrated in this otherwise awesome spectacle mounted by the Department of Trade and Commerce:

> Other nations, seeking to interpret the theme of the Fair, have concentrated on their national organizations for the health, happiness and security of their citizens. We are persuaded that in the World of Tomorrow the United States, the Scandinavian countries, Russia, England, Australia and even Italy, will be swell places to live in. They will all have healthy children, up-to-date equipment, beautiful cities, and a noble

> social philosophy. *Canada alone makes no reference whatsoever to the lives of its citizens*; the only [sic] equipment illustrated is railways, the only buildings are hotels and the only kind of recreation is that offered American tourists. There is much boasting of our abundant natural resources but no indication of how we intend to use them for the benefit of mankind in general and Canadians in particular.[20]

Any futuristic spectacle, especially one mounted by the state, is less prophetic than it is illustrative of current sociopolitical realities, including the prevailing ideology of those in power. The 1939 Canada Pavilion depicted Canada as virtually unpeopled and unclaimed ground—devoid of a citizenry who might figure into plans for the World of Tomorrow. The entirely abstract map and murals make no reference to an inhabiting populace who work and live in the country and thus have claims of their own on the territory. In an aside, the same reviewer noted that, of all the countries participating in the World's Fair, "Canada's is the only Pavilion that does not contain a Restaurant.... It was evidently foreseen that visitors would not wish to congregate here."[21] Even in this mundane oversight, the Pavilion conveyed an image of the country as unsettled and uninhabited, as a source of endless resources over which its citizens seemed to have no claim.

By the end of World War I and his work for the Rockefeller Foundation, Mackenzie King had come to believe that national economic development must give way to the emergent international "controlling units of economic organization".[22] As he wrote in *Industry and Humanity,* "In vain, national policies have striven to confine Industry within national bounds."[23] No doubt referring to Canada, he claimed that "government regulation has supplemented motives of patriotism in an endeavor to restrict foreign investments, but capital has proven as intractable as mercury, and has sought its returns in fields of promise wherever they lay."[24] Thus, multinational private enterprise "refuses to be hampered by restrictions; sooner or later it circumvents or overrides every obstacle in the path of prospective reward."[25] However, according to Mackenzie King, this characteristic of multinational industry should not be resisted, but "appreciated at its full value".[26] Because "the inherent ubiquity of capital sets limits to what may be possible under regulation, acquiesced in voluntarily or imposed by authority of the municipality, the state, or the nation," it was foolhardy to even think of intervening with regulations imposed by the state.[27]

Indeed, the inexorable course of U.S. multinational corporate enterprise was apparently God-given, and in the face of such manifest destiny, countries like Canada should sacrifice their own national economic development to serve a greater purpose. As he wrote three-quarters of the way through *Industry and Humanity,* "Each nation may yet find the salvation of its own industrial life by losing itself in an effort to save the industrial lives of other and rival nations. It is in such ways, through the course of time, that the economy of God gains world expression."[28]

True to his beliefs, the first two terms of Prime Minister Mackenzie King (1921-26 and 1926-30) were largely devoted to the "salvation" of Canada through the loss of its own economy. Encouraging the branch-plant expansion of U.S. multinationals across the country's "fields of promise", the Mackenzie King state worked doggedly and with missionary zeal to expand the economy of God and hasten its worldwide expression. This, of course, necessitated the consent of the Canadian public, and especially the consent of Canadian labour. According to the authors of *Twentieth Century Canada*,

> No decade was more disappointing for the Canadian labour movement than the 1920s. Throughout the twenties union membership plummeted in the face of an unparalleled antilabour onslaught by business. Organizers were blacklisted and fired; strikes fell into disuse as companies had armies of strike-breakers on hand to deal with any disruptions. Taking their cue from their counterparts in the United States, Candian employers began loudly demanding open shops and right-to-work laws which would bar unions from their plants. Others simply replaced unions with their own company unions. The crushing defeat of the Winnipeg General Strike [1919] had set a pattern for unholy alliances of business and government against unions all across Canada, but especially in the West. The labour movement was paralyzed, its leadership demoralized, its radicalism and vitality sapped.[29]

Sometimes consent to partnership in the economy of God needed a bit of a push.

With 80 per cent of the country's production from farms, forests, and mines sold outside its borders, Canada's dependent resource economy was, by the end of the 1920s, entirely vulnerable to any international economic instability.[30] The stock market crash of 1929 and the Depression hit Canada especially hard, as the demand for Canadian staples rapidly declined in the United States and elsewhere. But the crisis did not appear to shake the faith of Canada's political and business leaders in the economy of God. As John Herd Thompson writes in *Canada 1922-1939: Decades of Discord,* "Both the Conservative policy of higher tariffs and the Liberal alternative of freer trade deepened economic dependence on the United States. Between 1929 and 1935, the period at which the tariff was highest, the number of American branch plants operating in Canada increased from 524 to 816."[31]

With the dependent Canadian economy helping "to save the industrial lives of other and rival nations", the result for the Canadian public was a particularly grim "salvation". During the 1930s, one worker in three was without a job.[32] Mackenzie King's slogan during the election campaign in 1935, "King or Chaos", reflected his fears of widespread disillusionment, if not dissolution and incipient revolt. Once he returned to power, King's obsession became "the unity" of the country. As he declared in the House of Commons in March 1936, "I believe that Canada's first duty ... to the British Empire, with respect to all the great issues that come up, is, if possible, to keep this country united."[33]

But unity is not the same as nationhood. Indeed, as Tony Wilden states in *The Imaginary Canadian,* nationhood has been a "dirty word", a "forbidden word" in Canada because it conveys the potential of strength to resist colonization.[34] "Our colonial exploitation could not [be] accomplished without the active and passive collaboration of Canadians in positions of power," writes Wilden.[35] That collaboration during the 1920s and 1930s was finding its greatest expression in the building of north-south economic links with the United States, tying the country into those multinational "controlling units of economic organization" that Mackenzie King, and the country's colonial bourgeois powers, fully admired. In such a context, nationhood was a potential threat to the colonial structure, but "unity" carried another level of meaning.

In *The Bush Garden,* Northrop Frye writes:

> The famous Canadian problem of identity may seem a rationalized, self-pitying or made-up problem to those who have never had to meet it, or have never understood that it was there to be met. But it is with human beings as with birds: the creative instinct has a great deal to do with the assertion of territorial rights.[36]

Frye's link between "the problem of identity", "the creative instinct", and "the assertion of territorial rights" suggests that a people can have no national identity if they have no collective, boundaried claim to their own territorial ground. Colonization in its deepest, psychological sense is precisely the prevention of such identity and identified claim to place. Frantz Fanon's naming, in *The Wretched of the Earth,* of the constant question of the colonized—"In reality, who am I?"[37]—and Northrop Frye's pinpointing of the persistent Canadian riddle—"Where is here?"[38]—reveal essentially the same question writ from the different angles of identity and place.

The use of spectacle in a colonized context, as in the three state-arranged public-relations events of 1939, is devoted to addressing, rather than ignoring, the persistent riddle about identity and place. But the "answers" serve to re-articulate the status quo from which the riddle continually springs. In the Royal Visit and the royal ride along the QEW, the questions "Who are we?" and "Where is here?" are answered with reference to Great Britain and the United States; there is an identification with colonizing interests that perpetuates the problem of identity and the confusion of place. The Canadian Pavilion, presumably an occasion to answer the questions in Canadian terms, excluded Canada's own citizens from its national self-portrait, thereby revealing that its gleaming copper map had less to do with defining the finite boundaries of a nation than with depicting a nebulous territorial blur comprised of seemingly limitless expanses of natural resources.

In place of nationhood, then, the Canadian state was advocating unity. As Dallas W. Smythe observes in *Dependency Road,* "The rhetoric of Canadian federal politics has typically emphasized the need for, and even asserted the existence of, the unity or identity of people living in the country."[39] But, he notes, "The mere assertion of such a need passes as a surrogate for action to establish effectively such unity and identity—as a dozen or more reports by royal commissions created to investigate the need for various kinds of national policy attest."[40]

When rhetoric replaces effective action—especially action in service of Frye's "assertion of territorial rights"—then unity itself tends to exist primarily at the level of discourse. Any unravelling of that discourse threatens to make unity disappear, leaving exposed the collaborative measures that divide the country. In a similar fashion, any exposure of collaborative measures can be interpreted as an "attack on unity", with such nay-sayers perceived to be working against a united country. In this way, as Daniel Drache observed, "Leading the country meant playing off French against English, east against west, labour against business."[41] The colonial powers of business and government, in service to

Great Britain, the United States, and the branch-plant economy of God, could maintain their position through the 1920s and 1930s only with a policy of divide and rule. As Drache states, "national politics, when stripped of pretentious rhetoric, was a holding action where the centre be it Ottawa or Bay Street—that is the English majority, industry and finance—kept the nation 'together' by keeping it apart."[42]

That "holding action" of the Anglo-colonial majority transformed itself into a grip throughout the 1930s and into the first years of World War II, with extraordinary measures taken to ensure its maintenance. It is in this sense that Canada's immediate entry into World War II was inevitable. As John Herd Thompson argues,

> Despite the nationalists' loud protestations of autonomy and the many claims that Canada had become a North American nation, it was English Canada's sentimental attachment to the mother country that placed the country at Britain's side in 1939, not a revulsion against international fascism.[43]

Indeed, fascism had been alive and well in Canada for years. Hitler's rise to power, fuelled by anti-Semitism, anti-Bolshevism, and (after 1933) anti-trade unionism, had wide appeal to a variety of sectors in North American society. Hitler's hatred of Jews was virtually matched by his hatred of Slavs, whom he considered "the chaff of Europe" and a dangerous contaminant to the pure blood of the white races.[44] This view, in a less virulent form, was widespread in Canada in the prewar years, with many companies refusing to "knowingly hire a Jew, [or] anyone with a Ukrainian or Polish name".[45] James Gray writes: "ours was a society with a well-defined pecking order of prejudice. On the top were the race-proud Anglo-Saxons, who were prejudiced against everybody else. On the bottom were the Jews, against whom everybody discriminated."[46] Hitler's promise to crush what he perceived to be a Judeo-Communist worldwide conspiracy thus brought together under the fascist wing disparate segments of society during the 1930s.

For example, in 1936, attempts to mobilize a Canadian boycott of the Berlin Olympic Games were met with criticism, derision, and racial slurs from several mainstream Canadian newspapers.[47] For its part, Canada's hundred-member Olympic team, while marching past Hitler's box in the opening ceremonies, gave the Fuhrer the extended-arm Nazi salute—the only Commonwealth team to do so—claiming that it was "a gesture of friendship".[48] As well, the outbreak of the Spanish Civil War was met in Canada by legislation that threatened two years of imprisonment for those who volunteered to fight in Spain. Despite the Foreign Enlistment Act of 1937, some 600 Canadians joined the Mackenzie-Papineau Battalion of the International Brigade to fight for the Spanish Republic against Hitler and Franco.[49] To make its legislation appear even-handed, the Canadian government amended the Customs Act to forbid the sale of equipment or munitions for the struggle. The amendment, however, did not prevent Canada from selling indirectly to Franco through Morocco.[50]

In 1937, encouraged by British Prime Minister Neville Chamberlain, Mackenzie King was on his way to Germany to meet with the Fuhrer.[51] Chamberlain happened to be a major shareholder in Imperial Chemical Industries, a partner of I.G. Farben, Germany's petrochemical giant.[52] Mackenzie King was greatly impressed with Hitler, believing at the time that he "will rank some day with Joan of Arc among the deliverers of his people, & if he is only careful may yet be the deliverer of Europe".[53] Presumably, what Europe needed to be delivered from was the spectre of Bolshevism, if not the entire Judeo-Communist conspiracy.

As Austria and then Czechoslovakia toppled to Hitler's demands, assisted in part by Chamberlain's policy of appeasement, Mackenzie King remained hopeful about the Fuhrer's intentions. Following the Royal Visit to Canada, he decided to make another personal approach to Hitler. In the summer of 1939, Mackenzie King wrote to him:

> The purpose ... of this letter, is just to recall to your memory the conversation we had together, and to express anew the hope that regardless of what others may wish, or say, or do, you will, above all else, hold firm to the resolve not to let anything imperil or destroy what you have already accomplished, particularly for those whose lives are lived in humble circumstances.... I should like even more to say how much I hope that you will think not only of the good you can do for those of your own country, but that you will remember, as well, the good that you can do to the entire world. You will, I know, accept this letter in the spirit in which it is written—an expression of the faith I have in the purpose you have at heart.[54]

To his own diary, Mackenzie King confided his thoughts about the "forces unseen", the "loved ones in the beyond", who "were working for peace on earth" and in whose plan "it seemed to me Canada was being used as a screen to let friendly relations develop in a manner that would 'save face' as between Germany & Britain".[55]

The friendly relations between Germany and Britain had gone unimpeded in at least one area of international intercourse: "From 1933 up to the outbreak of World War II Hitler received tremendous financial aid from private British banks and the Bank of England itself."[56] But in the more public sphere of relations, the two countries were reaching an impasse. Mackenzie King's perception of Canada's role—as a "screen" to mediate between Britain and Germany and help them "save face"—was not unlike his vision of the country's role in relations between Great Britain and the United States. Apparently, cipher-like absence and supposedly selfless mediation were the proper lot of the country in troubled times.

Whatever the role of Mackenzie King's "unseen forces", war broke out between Great Britain and Germany on September 3, 1939, and within a week Canada had also declared war. A month later, the Canadian government decided to offer the post of Canada's first film commissioner to Grierson, who at the time was in Washington, D.C., conferring at length with the British ambassador to the United States, Lord Lothian. In her unpublished history of the National Film Board, Marjorie McKay explains the reasons for those discussions: "Britain was going to need all the understanding and help possible from the United States. Films about Britain and the British effort were needed for the widest possible distribution in the United States."[57]

In mid-October, Grierson accepted the post as Canada's film commissioner. The job was initially offered to him for a period of six months, but was ultimately extended until the end of World War II. As Gary Evans notes, "He remained on the payroll of Imperial Relations Trust until mid-1941. King's advisors knew Grierson was working for the British, though it is unlikely they knew the details of his assignment."[58] Grierson himself later wrote that "the Imperial Relations Trust had a lot to do originally with the setting up of the National Film Board in Canada", and called this "a fascinating incidental chapter in the total story".[59] Although Grierson encourages the assumption that the Trust's involvement was "incidental", it may account for several key decisions and practices instituted by him at the wartime NFB.

Thus, in the autumn of 1939, the fledgling National Film Board was faced with some peculiar and complex contradictions. From the perspective of the Canadian state and the dominant business community, it was to unite the country and serve "national purposes", without advocating nationhood. From the perspective of the National Film Act, it was to "interpret Canada to Canadians and to the world",[60] and at the same time, "diminish sectionalism". From the perspective of Mackenzie King, it might possibly provide "administrative machinery for the disposition of controversies" and help Canada be a mediating "screen" between world powers. From the perspective of the Imperial Relations Trust, it was to serve as a North American propaganda base, encouraging the United States to abandon its isolationist neutrality and reinforcing Canada in its partnership with Great Britain. With such varying perspectives to be reconciled, it is important to ask what kind of image of Canada could possibly emerge in the films?

Nonetheless, in 1939 the NFB looked to be, on the surface at least, an institution that might serve in place of the unfinished Trans-Canada Highway: an east-west interprovincial link. A better metaphor for Grierson's wartime NFB would be the Queen Elizabeth Way: a new north-south axis blessed by both Empires and paving the way for a greatly improved economy of God.

4

The Curse of Nations

I am of the scientific school myself and would leave less to chance in a hard and highly mobilized world.

JOHN GRIERSON

In September of 1939, Grierson had high hopes for his plan to establish an international film centre in the United States, which would distribute British documentary films across the country and thereby have an impact on public opinion in the former colony.[1] He submitted his plan to the British ambassador Lord Lothian, who forwarded it to Chamberlain's Ministry of Information. The ministry's reception of the plan was "frosty", and Grierson's hopes were dashed. As he wrote to Stephen Tallents at the Imperial Relations Trust: "I had this American job well sighted and could have done a valuable service. I could have commanded co-operation and even enthusiasm on this side on a large scale and, in one's own field, made the prevalent picture of a muddled and perhaps rather devious England clearer and more straightforward."[2] By October, he was "anxious to return to Britain", but accepted the Canadian offer to serve as film commissioner for six months because "he felt he could not stand aside and see the organisation he had created stillborn."[3]

In his 1938 report to the Canadian government, Grierson had proposed that "outside experts" be brought in to oversee film production, especially "in the case of prestige or documentary films".[4] Barely disguising his disdain for the scenic type of filmmaking engaged in by

Frank Badgley's Motion Picture Bureau, Grierson recommended that "the best associate producers available in Great Britain or the United States should be sought to begin with, preferably from Great Britain."[5]

True to his proposal, as well as to his assignment for Imperial Relations Trust, as film commissioner Grierson selected four other "outside experts" who, "between them, set the guidelines and established the working methods of the wartime National Film Board"[6]—Stuart Legg, Stanley Hawes, J.D. Davidson, and Raymond Spottiswoode. These filmmaking colleagues from the British documentary movement became the nucleus of the wartime NFB's production effort. Other appointments to the NFB in 1940 included secretary Janet Scellen, Evelyn Spice (from the General Post Office Film Unit), Ross McLean, Donald Fraser, James Beveridge (as filmmaking apprentices), and A. Phileas Côté to organize distribution.[7]

With its staff of ten, the NFB found itself in competition with Frank Badgley's Motion Picture Bureau and its more than 20 personnel apparently devoted to a very different conception of government filmmaking. The antagonism between Badgley and Grierson existed from the outset, although the reasons for that antagonism are not entirely clear. Gary Evans suggests that Grierson felt the bureau was too closely tied to one department (Trade and Commerce) and that the bureau's films did not have a broad, theatrical appeal.[8] Forsyth Hardy suggests that it was a case of an entrenched civil-servant mind-set resisting Grierson's dynamic ideas about film.[9] But there were also other factors.

In 1938, during his tour of Canada for the Imperial Relations Trust and the Canadian government, Grierson was asked what he thought of Canadian films, especially the work of the government's Motion Picture Bureau. He replied:

> I have seen many Canadian films and most of them were about National Parks and people on holidays. I didn't, so help me, believe that Canada could be just the big innocent, baby-hearted, holiday haunt it pretended to be in its pictures. I thought maybe somebody did some work once in a while and that Canada's work might just conceivably have something to do with the real Canada. That in fact is my interest in the world. I would like to see more and more films about real people.[10]

It is an interesting reponse, especially considering Paul Rotha's complaint that Grierson's films of the 1930s were inevitably about machines and the people behind the machines, people no one ever gets to know.

Nevertheless, Grierson's primary interest was in stark contrast to the Badgley Bureau's emphasis on scenic filmmaking.

The antagonism between Grierson and Badgley reached a crisis stage in November 1940. Feeling strongly that the Motion Picture Bureau should be brought under the administration of the National Film Board, Grierson decided to force the issue by submitting his resignation.[11] To his colleague Basil Wright in Britain, he wrote:

> I'm due to depart from here at the end of January [1941]. I have given them hell over the year, meaning mostly Frank Badgley and his veterans. I've been sorry to do it, and in a small town like this it seems almost sadistic; but it was a case of either / or. Frank could neither see the purposes, nor had the energy for the required initiative....[12]

Grierson in 1940 was by no means devoid of opportunities to exercise his considerable propagandistic talents. He was still under hire to the Imperial Relations Trust and in fact had spent much of the year travelling in that capacity. His Film Centre in London was a thriving concern, partly as a result of the reorganization of the Ministry of Information just in advance of the change in government from Chamberlain to Churchill. The new head of the films division of Britain's Ministry of Information was Grierson's old friend Jack Beddington, general manager and director of publicity for Shell–Mex BP.[13] As a result of Beddington's appointment in 1940, "the documentary movement got the kind of leadership it wanted".[14] As Basil Wright later recalled, Grierson's Film Centre "was as big and as powerful as the Crown film unit in relation to the Ministry of Information during the war".[15] Moreover, the Rockefeller Foundation had kicked in some money so that the Film Centre could begin publishing the *Documentary News Letter* in January 1940, with Grierson on the editorial board.[16] All things considered, Grierson's prospects looked just fine on the eve of 1941. He was not about to let a provincial civil servant like Frank Badgley rain on his parade.

The terms on which Grierson would stay in Canada were quite clear: any decision to stay, he asserted, "must depend on the creation of a state of confidence regarding fundamental points of policy".[17] Evidence of that "state of confidence" depended on the government making two administrative changes: putting the Bureau under the administration of the NFB, and enabling the Board to "relate its creative needs" directly to the Treasury.[18]

For seven and a half months, the issues of these terms were bandied about the corridors of power, until finally Mackenzie King used his authority to break the log jam.[19] On June 11, 1941, Grierson took over the Motion Picture Bureau and its staff; he was able to transfer the NFB out from under the minister of Trade and Commerce to a new minister of national war services, J.T. Thorson, and was given the authority to hire non-civil-service personnel for the NFB on a per job basis.[20] It was a decisive turning-point for the NFB. Unfortunately, Frank Badgley, the loser in the stand-off, died within a year, his already poor health aggravated by personal problems. "Grierson, never one to hold a personal grudge, went to visit Badgley in the hospital shortly before he died."[21]

The new terms of reference for the NFB in 1941 made a dramatic difference, especially in the "creative manpower" that Grierson had found so lacking in the Bureau's civil-service veterans. Now able to hire on a three-month or per job basis, Grierson proceeded to call in an impressive host of other "outside experts". As one wartime filmmaking participant put it, "Soon the international character of the [NFB] staff ... began to assert itself with increasing vigour."[22] Even a short-list of visiting documentarians hired temporarily by the wartime Board is impressive: Basil Wright, Joris Ivens, Irving Jacoby, Roger Barlow, Nicholas Read, Robert Flaherty, John Ferno, Boris Kaufman, Alexander Alexieff, Henri Storck, Helen Lewis.

By contrast, Grierson's selection of Canadians for the NFB seems to have centred around those with absolutely no experience in film. With the exception of individuals like Evelyn Spice, Julian Roffman, Leo Setzer (Canadians working in film outside the country), Grierson was primarily interested in young Canadian apprentices who had no knowledge of the medium. Even more specifically, as Stuart Legg recalled, "If they said all they really wanted to do was make movies, they weren't hired."[23]

Perhaps this selection of Candian neophytes coincided with a need for a kind of filmmaking *tabula rasa* on which Grierson could impose his propaganda style. As he later wrote, "The British Documentary School did not stay at home but, because of its nature, spread abroad and particularly to those countries where the need for it was most deeply rooted (in young countries like Canada ...)."[24] Then again, the need for absolute neophytes may have coincided with Grierson's plan that the wartime NFB would make a good number of its films, and most of its "prestige" films, without the use of the camera. As Julian Roffman observed about the Canadian apprentices, "They were all wildly engaged in making films, but none of them knew which end of the camera took the picture...."[25]

Sometime between October 1939 and April 1940, Grierson and his production supervisor Stuart Legg decided that the wartime NFB would primarily make compilation films, films incorporating secondhand footage procured from other sources. Gary Evans explains this decision as having been "dictated by the urgency of war and lack of time",[26] but there may have been other factors involved. Grierson hinted, in a letter to Stephen Tallents, at what could be gained by this choice of technique:

> There has been a good deal of thought and research behind the films and of a more deliberate and scientific nature than we ever got organised for in England.... We have certainly diverged a long way from the documentary model now being pursued in England: in the direction of more knowledge of political plan and the design behind the news.[27]

In other words, the manipulation of secondhand footage afforded a greater degree of "deliberate and scientific" control over the persuasive message. Coupled with a voice-of-authority soundtrack, these films could be more precisely designed, their propagandist intent more sharply controlled. By contrast, on-location shooting left the filmmaking process open to a greater degree of chance.

Grierson, the propaganda maestro, was not about to risk his opportunity for the manufacture of consent by indulging the NFB in extensive shooting. As he wrote, "I am of the scientific school myself and would leave less to chance in a hard and highly mobilized world."[28] Grierson believed that "The problems of a modern highly developed industrial economy involve the creative action of the community operating as a single, integrated and unified force".[29] To achieve this end, he recognized that a scientific planning of information would be better served by the compilation technique.

It is at least feasible that this production decision was a factor in the antagonism between Badgley and Grierson. Grierson's complaining letter to Basil Wright, written in the midst of his temporary resignation from his commissioner's post, mentions "the forty films made in the first year of the Board, compared with the one and a half made by the Motion Picture Bureau".[30] Clearly, such an output, though impressive, depended primarily on using the much faster compilation method of production, especially given a staff of ten at the time. The compilation technique may well have been part of Badgley's quarrel with Grierson's NFB. Whatever the case, this production decision was also a political decision, since it had immediate and long-term repercussions for Canada.

The "highest priority" for Grierson and Legg at the wartime NFB was the "prestige" series, "Canada Carries On" and "World in Action", both of which used the compilation technique.[31] The "Canada Carries On" series, created for both domestic and international exhibition, was launched in April 1940, with Stuart Legg as producer and a "team proper" comprised of apprentices Tom Daly, Gordon Wiesenborn, and Margaret Ann Adamson (Lady Elton).[32] Other Canadian apprentices, hired "if they showed an intellectual agility and background similar to Grierson's", included Stanley Jackson, James Beveridge, Donald Fraser, Sydney Newman, Morten Parker, Michael Spencer, Gudrun Bjerring (Parker), Daphne Lilly (Anstey), and Jane Marsh (Beveridge).[33] With monthly releases, "Canada Carries On" eventually included some 62 films, which were intended to articulate Canada's role in the war effort and its place in international geopolitics. Grierson arranged for distribution of "Canada Carries On" films by Columbia Pictures for the Canadian market, Paramount Pictures for the British market, and Fox Films for Australia and New Zealand.[34] After their theatrical release, many of the films in the series were then re-released for distribution on the non-theatrical rural circuits set up by the NFB in 1942.

The second "prestige" series, "The World in Action", had Grierson as its producer and Stuart Legg as its writer-director for all but three of some 30 films.[35] Launched in 1942, the series was intended to be "the voice of Canada" on international events: to articulate a Canadian geopolitical vision on the screens of the United States and the United Kingdom through distribution by United Artists.[36] Primarily the work of Grierson and Legg, the series had a number of Canadian apprentices and assistants working on production, including James Beveridge, Jane Marsh, and Tom Daly.[37]

In both series, original footage was limited and often non-existent. "Canada Carries On" used some original footage but most of what appeared on the screen was obtained from secondary sources.[38] "The World in Action" was almost entirely comprised of compilation footage. Using stock-shots, footage supplied by other sources, and film sequences taken out of other newsreels and documentaries, both series depended on the skills of film editing and the use of voice-over narration to provide coherence to the image-track.

The film footage for these compilation shorts came from a wide variety of commercial and non-commercial sources. Grierson obtained footage from Jack Beddington's Film Unit in the British Ministry of

Information, from the U.S. Signal Corps, and from the Free French newsreel unit.[39] Within a short time, he obtained access to all official British and American film footage for recutting and use with NFB productions.[40] He was also appointed Canada's Custodian of Enemy Films, and in that capacity he was able continually to secure extensive enemy film footage captured by the Allies, footage from Germany, Italy, and Japan.[41] Grierson made arrangements with Paramount Films for the NFB to take sequences and shots from their weekly French newsreel, "Actualités Olympiques".[42] And he lined up NFB access to commercial stock-shot libraries in the United States. As Gary Evans notes, "Film Board employees, soon called 'pirates' ... became proficient at locating material from the Pathe and Fox Movietone libraries in New York."[43]

With this wealth of footage from other sources, as well as from the stock-shot library of the government's Motion Picture Bureau, employees at the NFB were thus busily involved in the reassembly and re-editing of secondhand material—and not just newsreels and stock-shots. Foreign documentary works like *Industrial Britain,* Riefenstahl's *Triumph of the Will,* Eisenstein's *October,* and Humphrey Jennings' *Listen to Britain* were just a few of the productions recut and reused in NFB wartime compilation films, and usually there was no credit given to the original filmmakers. Grierson also adopted the practice of not indicating in the films the extent to which captured enemy footage had been incorporated. Apparently, "he did not think it was in the public interest to know."[44]

Julian Roffman's observation that the Canadian apprentices were "wildly engaged in making films" although "none of them knew which end of a camera took the picture" was thus no exaggeration. Although the NFB later engaged in original shooting for some of the films used on the non-theatrical circuits, in terms of the "prestige" series for theatrical distribution at home and abroad, there was little need for the Canadian apprentices to know how to operate a movie camera. The bulk of the work was research, "pirating" (the location of stock-footage in others' libraries), neg-cutting, editing, scripting, as well as the meticulous cataloguing of all this on-going accumulation of secondhand footage.

It seems, in retrospect, a curious production decision, especially given that Mackenzie King had provided Grierson with "almost a blank cheque in support" of his plans for the National Film Board.[45] Presumably, the prime minister's blank cheque and personal backing might have allowed the wartime NFB to readily engage in extensive shooting across Canada, to purchase updated sound-film equipment, and to use original footage in its "prestige" films. Certainly it seems fair to ask just what kind of "voice of Canada" was expected to emerge from Grierson's choice of the compilation technique, especially given another of his decisions: "Our policy ... when we send Canadian films abroad is to invite the countries receiving them to remake them in their own style and use their own editorial comment."[46]

Significantly, as Gary Evans has pointed out, the compilation technique was one which Grierson, in the late 1920s, had ruled out as unsuitable for the British documentarians.[47] During his pre–World War II career, Grierson had produced dozens of films, but had directed only two: *Drifters* in 1928, using on-location shooting, and *Conquest,* a 1929 experiment with the compilation technique. In *Conquest,* using film clips from Badgley's Motion Picture Bureau and from Hollywood features like *The Covered Wagon, The Iron Horse,* and *Pony Express,* Grierson attempted through compilation to make a film (ironically enough) "on the pioneering development of Canada".[48] The result quickly led him to recognize that the compilation technique had significant limitations. Though both on-location shooting and compilation were "consciously persuasive", the latter technique afforded the filmmaker less artistic control and creative scope.[49] Thus, "Grierson chose to develop the British documentary film along the lines of *Drifters* rather than those of *Conquest*", opting for on-location shooting rather than for the technique of "manipulating dated newsreel or stock footage".[50] By choosing the compilation technique for Canada's wartime "prestige" production, the creation of imagery seems to have been consciously sacrificed. Though deemed not good enough for the British documentaries of the 1930s, the compilation film became the hallmark of the NFB's wartime production style.

While compilation gave Grierson and Legg (who oversaw all production for both series) a greater degree of "deliberate and scientific" control, it also was a technique better suited for conveying Grierson's internationalist vision to Canadian audiences. One result of compiling an image-track from multiple sources and a variety of countries' screen output was that any given film in "Canada Carries On" or "The World in Action" was typically a kaleidoscopic collage of places all around the world. As wartime filmmaker Ernst Borneman observed about NFB films in general at the time, "The visual by itself constantly skipped from place to place all over the globe".[51] This "global" vision in the image-track corresponded with the viewpoint that Grierson strongly advocated for Canada:

> Canada is waking up to her place in the world and is conscious, as few English-speaking countries seem to be, that it is a new sort of place in the world.... Canada is moving swiftly towards a world viewpoint as England in recent years has been moving away from it.[52]

This "world viewpoint" was part of Grierson's political and economic vision and his belief that multinational corporations could bring order to economic chaos. Sensing that England was missing "the boundary-crossings in economic terms of world events", that it was not perceiving "the need for new economic integration", and was in fact moving away from a "world viewpoint" during the war, Grierson undertook to preach his internationalist perspective to Canadians whose territory had already been long colonized by multinational branch plants.[53] Because such a perspective could not be voiced directly without alienating important sectors in Canada (as well as his socialist-thinking colleagues within the British documentary movement), Grierson was always careful to couch his position in vague terms, an approach that would eventually backfire on him in the postwar years.

Nevertheless, his advocacy of a "world viewpoint" for Canada had significant repercussions for this country, especially for its postwar film and media policy. During the war, one immediate result can be found in production practices. More than ten years after the introduction of sound-equipment for filmmaking, virtually the only use of sound in wartime NFB prestige films was the insistent, lone voice-of-authority and the incessant musical counterpoint. The combination of "international" image-track and voice-of-authority soundtrack was to prove quite useful to Grierson's political intent, especially in deflecting any impulses towards Canadian nationalism.

The war years, especially 1939-43, were years of extraordinary change for the country. In the summer of 1939, Canada was primarily an agricultural country, importing most of its machine tools, chemicals, and manufactured goods from Great Britain and the United States. Under the pressures of mobilization for the war, and particularly through the fully centralized power of the government's Department of Munitions and Supply (administered by C.D. Howe), Canada transformed its previous agrarian-based position virtually overnight, becoming a major supplier of both manufactured goods and foodstuffs.

> In four years (1939-1943) the Dominion had undergone an industrial transformation which under normal circumstances might well have

> taken half a century or more. Some $800 million had been spent on hundreds of new plants and their facilities.... In four years, more than $1,380,000,000 was spent on industrial construction....[54]

This profound transformation of Canada's industrial position was accompanied by another potentially significant change in the country's standing with both Great Britain and the United States. By borrowing from the Canadian people through the sale of war bonds, the country reduced its external debt by 54 per cent, while increasing its internal debt some 260 per cent.[55] Canada's energies were thus being devoted to two significant conversions: from industrial dependency on external sources to increased industrial self-sufficiency; and from financial indebtedness to foreign sources to financial reliance on internal sources of capital.

Because of the branch-plant nature of the Canadian economy, however, such changes did not necessarily mean any great leap forward in economic independence. Indeed, government-financed expansion of U.S.-based corporate enterprise benefitted those companies tremendously. Nonetheless, these changes in Canada's industrial / financial position at least contained the potential for a greater degree of self-determination. Perhaps even more significant, the concerted effort of the Canadian people not only was providing the country with both manufactured and resource goods, but was also supplying Great Britain with extraordinary support.

War historian C.P. Stacey has estimated that Canada's total assistance to Britain throughout the war—in the form of goods shipped, the "billion-dollar gift", and Mutual Aid—amounted to $3,043,000,000.[56] None of this was expected to be repaid. By comparison to U.S. assistance to Great Britain, Canada's wartime contribution, in per capita terms, was fully three times higher.[57] Considering this wartime effort and generosity of Canadians and this significant reversal in the dependent relationship with Great Britain, one would expect to find the Canadian documentary films produced in such a context resonating with nationalistic pride and healthy self-consciousness. But as Ernst Borneman noted at the time, with reference to both "Canada Carries On" and "The World in Action" series:

> [Stuart] Legg and his team presented the strategic history of total war on the screens of Canada, and the very understatement of the Canadian part in total battle served to bring home the message of humility ... with greater insistence than any pat-on-the-back production could ever have done.[58]

Besides this "understatement of the Canadian part in total battle" and a "message of humility", there is an underlying motif in many of the films that could be called an anxiety about Canadian nationalism. Grierson's position was that Canada should "forget nationalism", and the "world viewpoint" of both prestige series was itself a way of pointing away from Canada, of downplaying the Canadian role in the war.[59] The title of the series "Canada Carries On" might suggest a focus on Canada as the subject of exploration, though this was not necessarily the case, as films in the series like "Britain at Bay", "Everywhere in the World", "Churchill's Island", "This is Blitz", "Geopolitik—Hitler's Plan for Europe", "Road to Tokyo", "Fighting Norway", "Gates of Italy" indicate.

At times, the anxiety about nationalism becomes explicit. For example, Grierson's favourite documentary from this period, *The War for Men's Minds* (1943), argues forcefully against "the fanatics whose religion was narrow nationalism", thus equating Nazism with any form of nationalist thinking. The discussion-trailer accompanying the film *Battle is the Birthright* (1943) is even more specific. Intended to spur local discussion among viewers on the non-theatrical rural circuits, this trailer at the end of the film includes the following exchange among panel members:

> *Jane Marsh* (NFB film director): Do you remember a scene in the picture of a Nazi party conference? There we saw men dedicating themselves to one man. Instead of that, shouldn't young Canadians dedicate themselves to Canada?
>
> *Bill Rennett* (National Research Council): That would be ultra-nationalism! No way out for the future at all.
>
> *Captain Feisenchon* (Canada Youth Training Program): Well then, let them dedicate themselves to the cause of the common people.
>
> *Moderator*: Or, as the film said, our young men realize that they have to give the kids a better chance, help them to develop a sound mind and a sound body. That means better schooling and more time for recreation.
>
> *Feisenchon*: Yes, it's very important that the men at the front and the civilians at home understand that there are two battles. We're fighting now to defeat the enemy. After the war we have to struggle for a better society.
>
> *Rennett*: Not a nationalist society, a better society for all people.
>
> *Moderator*: So a film forum begins. Why not start one here tonight, too?

Equating "young Canadians dedicating themselves to Canada" with "ultra-nationalism", and the association of that aspiration with Nazism, was surely an effective way of discouraging nationalism. None of the other panelists challenged this view, and the last word on the subject is given to the panel member most insistent that Canadians should avoid nationalistic notions.

Whether this was the view of the Canadian filmmaking apprentices under Grierson's wartime tutelage is not at all obvious. The NFB history written by Marjorie McKay in the mid-1960s reveals a lingering ambivalence about the nationalistic views of those Canadians (including McKay herself) working for Grierson during the war. At one point she writes: "Canadian nationalism isn't a phenomenon of the sixties. It was present and just as strong in the forties. Not that the Canadians at the Board did not give Grierson the hero worship and idolatry reserved usually for more holy characters."[60] But just four pages before this assertion, her text reads: "Few [Canadians at the wartime NFB] had any mental concept of Canada as a country with national goals. The Canadian consciousness existed in a very few minds in those years."[61]

Perhaps this textual ambivalence is itself representative of the state of consciousness during the war years, an ambivalence that, in the case of the young filmmaking apprentices, must be placed in juxtaposition to "hero worship" towards a film mentor whose own views about Canadian nationalism were not at all ambivalent. As Gary Evans notes, Grierson "kept his own personal pipeline to individual young filmmakers to jive them up and stimulate them and give them his own sense of perspective".[62]

Whether the young filmmakers knew it or not, that perspective against nationalism extended even to a policy recommendation from the film commissioner to the government, arguing that Canada should not attempt in the postwar years to develop its own film industry. As he wrote in his 1944 "Film Policy for Canada":

> As we become more and more an important nation in the world, must we build our own film industry as an expression of our own life and a safeguard of our own national identity? Or is this just old-fashioned nationalistic nonsense? Is it not the curse of nations that everyone of them should be so insistent on its own unique and special virtues? Isn't there another world of loyalty, faith and pride in which national barriers do not mean a thing?[63]

But in more immediate terms, Grierson's internationalist effort against "old-fashioned nationalistic nonsense" was having its effect on the films and filmmakers under his wartime tutelage. The "curse of nations" was not about to strike either of his "prestige" series. The compilation film would see to that.

Biographer Forsyth Hardy provides an interesting anecdote that illuminates some of the effects of Grierson's production decision on the resulting film ethos. There were three film specialists in the immediate Grierson family, though John's sisters Marion and Ruby are rarely remembered. Before her death at sea in a torpedoed ship in 1940, Ruby Grierson had directed a number of documentary films with a style and flair that brought her admiring attention. Hardy recounts a dialogue that occurred between the two siblings just before the making of the film *Housing Problems* in mid-1930s Britain, a film usually attributed to Arthur Elton and Edgar Anstey.

Ruby Grierson's views on documentary film and on the role of filmmakers were radically different from those of brother John.

> 'The trouble with you', she said to her brother, 'is that you look at things as though they were in a goldfish bowl.' Grierson: 'Yes I do. But so what?' Ruby Grierson: 'I'm going to break your goldfish bowl.' And so Ruby said to the slum-dwellers in *Housing Problems*: 'The camera is yours. The microphone is yours. Now tell the bastards exactly what it's like to live in slums.'[64]

The film was a sensation for its time. It abandoned the standard technique of using a post-recorded "voice-of-God" narration in which a single voice of authority, inevitably middle-class male, expounds throughout the film on the situation explored in the images. Instead, *Housing Problems* incorporated the cockney voices of its screen subjects, telling about their situation from their own point of view and in their own words. This forerunner of "cinema direct" (though a goldfish bowl of another sort) was precisely the model that Grierson avoided for Canada, though ironically the first two films produced in Canada under his official aegis came close to it.

While Grierson was drafting the National Film Act in 1938-39, the minister of labour asked him to recommend someone to make two films on the government's youth-training program.[65] In February 1939, Grierson suggested that Stuart Legg be brought to Canada to make the films, which became *Youth for Tomorrow* and *The Case of Charlie Gordon*. Both productions involved extensive location shooting. For *Youth for Tomorrow* Legg and his crew travelled from Glace Bay to the

Peace River, and for *The Case of Charlie Gordon* they shot in small-town Nova Scotia. The latter film in its final form focussed on the personal story of one unemployed youth's life. Told from Charlie Gordon's point of view, with some re-enactments of personal situations, the film contained elements of both cinema direct and docu-drama. But more important, both of these films—in their image-track and their soundtrack—explored specifically Canadian themes and subjects.

With the official founding of the NFB and the onset of war, however, this strand of filmmaking gave way to what was deemed a more important focus:

> Legg himself began to dissociate himself more and more definitely from the 'drama-on-your-doorstep' mentality and began to develop the "Canada Carries On" and "World in Action" technique of editorial internationalism which was to become one of Canada's major contributions to documentary.... From the beginning of the series, Legg had considered it fully within the scope of his work to examine countries other than Canada on a social, economic, and political basis....[66]

The compilation technique and the focus on editorial internationalism had long-term repercussions for both Canadian filmmakers and viewers.

First, we might consider the "international" image-track a contribution to Northrop Frye's persistent Canadian riddle: "Where is here?" Both "Canada Carries On" and "The World in Action" visually convey dislocation, a kaleidoscopic confusion of locale. A national cinema, by framing scenes and images of a country, helps to establish the boundaries of that nation, to convey a sense of place. The viewer becomes steeped in a familiar, boundaried, cinematic "here". The importance of that centredness has been recognized by Margaret Atwood, who writes: "A person who is 'here' but would rather be somewhere else is an exile or a prisoner; a person who is 'here' but thinks he is somewhere else is insane."[67] In those terms, the two wartime "prestige" series conveyed a confused "nowhere", a boundaryless and restless absence of place.

On a more political level, we must consider the image-track of these compilation films as essentially colonized. Though Grierson defined documentary film as "the creative treatment of actuality", in the Canadian wartime NFB context, it would be more accurate to define the methods as the creative treatment of footage from "elsewhere". If, as Evans suggests, NFB employees earned the soubriquet of "pirates", we must also apply the term to the adoption of others' points of view through the obtained images. While the wartime "prestige" series subtly served to deliver a "message of humility" and an underlying anxiety about nationalism to Canadian viewers, on some level the filmmaking apprentices themselves were being trained in "humility", to consider "here" as unimportant, to think of any Canadian "drama-on-your-doorstep" as essentially inferior. They would tend to become increasingly divorced from the real concerns of their own locale, would be more philosophically oriented, and less inclined to adopt a personal or committed position. The tendency would be to approach things from a highly dispassionate, intellectualized stance, which could encompass multiple points of view on a subject. Such a "world viewpoint" would also rule out personal or national themes and topics.

Film scholar Peter Harcourt recognized these qualities in many of the 1960s documentaries made 20 years later by the English-speaking side of the NFB. In analyzing some of the work of Unit B, Harcourt identifies qualities of an "abstract and slightly rhetorical air", a lack of personal urgency, a lack of "autobiographical charge". He writes:

> There is in all these films a quality of suspended judgment, of something left open at the end, of something undecided. And if one thinks of the films of Franju, Marker or Vas, of their insistently personal quality, there is also something academic about the way the Canadian films have been conceived. There is something rather detached from the immediate pressures of existence, something rather apart.[68]

Although Harcourt suggests that these qualities in the films are "very Canadian", they might be traced back to Grierson's wartime influence and his schooling of Canadian apprentices (including Unit B's Tom Daly and Colin Low) in compilation films and a "world viewpoint". Harcourt himself provides a clue to such a tracing when he mentions Humphrey Jennings's war documentaries:

> The sharpest foil would be Humphrey Jennings and his films about the war. Jennings was a man who to a large extent had the personal quality of his films thrust upon him by the conditions of his time. He also experienced, both in his films and in his life, an immediacy of contact with his fellow men, and a certainty of identity in relation to the world in which he lived.[69]

It was precisely the films by Humphrey Jennings—especially *London Can Take It* (1940) and *Listen to Britain* (1941)—that Grierson found irritatingly sentimental, passive examples of wartime British cinema.[70] As part of his training of the Canadian filmmaking apprentices during the war, Grierson used the work of Jennings to illustrate what the NFB documentaries should *not* be like.[71]

It may have been those very qualities of a personal and localized approach in Jennings's films, or even what Harcourt has called "a certainty of identity", that Grierson considered inappropriate for the NFB, since he was interested in the elimination of national barriers and "old-fashioned nationalistic nonsense", the avoidance of any so-called "romantic" notion of personal or national viewpoint.[72]

Thus, it is possible to question whether the characteristics of abstraction, suspended judgment, indecision, detachment, and lack of a personal or emotional charge in some of the later English NFB productions were "very Canadian" or were the lingering influence of Grierson and Legg's tutelage. Comparing some of the Unit B films with French-Canadian documentaries of the same 1960s period, Harcourt notes:

> The French-speaking films seem less concerned with subjects that open out upon some worldwide interest ... than they are to depict minutely some little-known aspect of French-Canadian life. 'This is how we live,' films such as *Les Raquetteurs* or *Les Bucherons de la Manouane* seem to be saying, 'this is what all the trouble is about, for this is what we want to be allowed to develop, this is what we wish to preserve.' Films such as *A Saint Henri, Le 5 Septembre* (1961) or the highly-praised *Pour la Suite du Monde* (1962), while certainly moving social documents, most lovingly observed, lack any reference outwards to the larger world beyond Quebec.[73]

Grierson hired very few Québecois in a filmmaking capacity during the war years, and as D.B. Jones states in his history of the NFB, "the major French-Canadian work in the wartime Film Board was the versioning of English-language films into French...."[74] Quite apart from the discrimination involved, perhaps this exclusion prevented the Griersonian "world viewpoint" from having any lingering influence on postwar Quebec filmmakers.

By the time of the Quiet Revolution, Quebec documentarians were interested in the particularities of their own milieu, the exploration of what was "unique and special" about their own context and locale. As part of decolonization, such a viewpoint is obviously the foil to a sense of inferiority and humility about one's place in the scheme of things. Pride of self and place, focussing on a unique culture and language, were obviously part of the social movement for self-determination and sovereignty. By contrast, many Anglophone filmmakers of the same period retained the tendency to have their documentary films "open out upon some world-wide interest", thereby avoiding exploration of English Canada. Harcourt phrases this somewhat differently, as the propensity to "contemplate the Great Problems of our Age", but this can be seen as the old lure of Griersonian internationalism reaching ever more abstract heights:

> "What is a number that a man may know it and a man that he may know a number?" ... It is the presence of [such] questions, veering constantly towards the ultimate, that give the films their abstract and slightly rhetorical air, as they give them that quality which might strike Europeans as a boyish sense of wonder.[75]

Although the wartime compilation films and editorial internationalism had lingering effects on English-Canadian documentary, these emphases may also have had repercussions for fictional films. Both the technique and the "world viewpoint" in "Canada Carries On" and "The World in Action" moved audiences and filmmakers away from the "drama-on-your-doorstep" mentality so necessary to fictional narrative. Peter Morris suggests that the "quintessential Canadian film form" throughout the sporadic history of Canadian cinema since the turn of the century, has been the dramatized documentary or docu-drama.[76] At the wartime NFB, the relegation of original shooting to a secondary role meant that only a few films in the "prestige" series—for example, Julian Roffman's *Thirteen Platoon* (1942) and Robert Edmond's *Coal Face, Canada* (1943)—were structured around narrative components, though other films, like Joris Ivens's *Action Stations!* and Jane Marsh's *Proudly She Marches,* contain moments of docu-drama.[77] The move away from story-line to geopolitical rhetoric for a more "deliberate and scientific" design may have hindered the development of docu-drama as well.

Whatever its many faults, Frank Badgley's Motion Picture Bureau had at least focussed its attention on Canada, conveying through its scenics some sense of place. Under Grierson's tutelage, the tendency to look everywhere else but here for important themes and drama was reinforced for audiences and filmmakers alike. Grierson's lessons in "editorial internationalism" made the finding of the national doorstep more difficult.

In such a wartime context, it would be surprising not to find intimations of rebellion among the Canadian filmmakers themselves. According to Marjorie McKay, by at least 1944 some of the Canadians at the NFB had begun to question the state of things under the propaganda maestro. Sydney Newman and Guy Glover, who had worked for the "Canada Carries On" series in a variety of compilation roles, "argued with Grierson ... and claimed that the Canadian content was lacking".[78] As McKay puts it, "The old resentment of the English was as strong as ever among the Canadians", who were apparently growing tired of their subservient role to the "outside experts".[79] Moreover, "Canadian filmmakers wanted to select subjects for films and determine what should be done in them."[80] Such observations further indicate the colonized position of the NFB under Grierson and Legg, who together retained full editorial control. As a result of the initiative by Newman and Glover, "Canada Carries On", after four years of British dominance, was handed over to its two new coproducers, Newman and Glover, for the last year of the war.

The fate of another upstart Canadian filmmaker was less propitious. According to Barbara Martineau, wartime filmmaker Jane Marsh was the "obvious choice" to fill a role as producer for "Canada Carries On" in advance of the initiative by Newman and Glover. Having compiled a number of films for the series—*Inside Fighting Canada* (1942), *Women Are Warriors* (1942), *Proudly She Marches* (1943), *Air Cadets* (1944), one entry for "The World in Action" series, *Wings on Her Shoulder* (1943), and a film for the non-theatrical circuits, *Alexis Tremblay, Habitant,* Marsh had a feel for what might be accomplished. But "Grierson didn't want a woman as producer of that series."[81] During their confrontation, Grierson announced his decision to cut the length of the films by half and release twice as many films each month. Marsh argued that the quality of the films for "Canada Carries On" would be destroyed by such a move, and to make her point she resigned in protest. "To her chagrin, Grierson accepted her resignation."[82] This power play, enacted around the issue of film length, thereby avoided the deeper issue of sexism and Grierson's reluctance to have a woman produce a "prestige" series. Grierson's sexism has been noted by Ruth Roach Pierson in *Canadian Women and the Second World War*:

> [O]f the nearly one hundred people employed in film production at the height of the war, only three or four women rose to prominence as directors and producers. The largest proportion of women were employed as secretaries, stenographers, and librarians, and as negative cutters....[83]

This was, in fact, an improvement over Grierson's attitude during the 1930s, when the "monastic" discipline he imposed on his film units meant that even filmmakers' wives were barred from the premises.[84] By World War II Grierson's sexism was at least the equivalent of his British paternalism. In this sense, there is another way to view his reluctance to have Jane Marsh as a producer for "Canada Carries On".

Marsh's films have a tendency to articulate a point of view that is not quite "editorial internationalism". Her films are neither entirely self-effacing nor fully impersonal, as so many of the "prestige" series films markedly are. Rather, her films incorporate irony and humour, a budding feminist perspective and perhaps more important, they consistently focus on Canadian subjects and locales. Ironically, in addition to being a woman, she held a perspective that Grierson may have considered too Canadian for "Canada Carries On". As Gary Evans writes, "In the final analysis the 'Canada Carries On' series succeeded by concentrating primarily upon trying to place Canada in relation to world events and the global struggle of war, and avoided falling back upon nationalism and parochial issues."[85] As a producer heading up the series, Marsh might have undermined such success.

Grierson's political stand against Canadian nationalism and for a "world viewpoint", reinforced by the choice of the compilation technique, has rarely been challenged or criticized. In his 1984 text on the wartime NFB, Gary Evans tends to adopt Grierson's position. He writes:

> One of the new attitudes which the war had fostered was the acknowledgement of the interdependency of nations on a scale never before realized. It was this new reality which both Grierson and Legg hoped would replace the old nationalism which had been partly responsible for both world wars. If people and governments could be convinced that an era of international brotherhood was to follow the war there would indeed be a brave new world. Obviously, the alternative was World War III and the end of civilization.[86]

Evans's closing sentence tends to mask some significant aspects of this perspective.

First of all, as of the outbreak of World War II, Canada had yet to experience "the old nationalism" which Grierson and Legg were so adamantly against. In the wartime 1940s, the changes in Canada's relationship with Great Britain and the United States, at least in its production and financial status, might well have led to Canadians becoming conscious of their country as a "unique and special" nation whose boundaries deserved strengthening and protection. More importantly, such a consciousness is necessary for a national identity and an authentic voice as a separate country. Although Grierson perceived this insistence on a separate and unique identity as "the curse of nations", it is by no means the cause of war. Rather, it could be argued that the failure to respect and tolerate national boundaries causes wars.

Second, the "acknowledgement of the interdependency of nations" does not necessarily exclude nationalism. On the contrary, it is possible to maintain that such interdependency actually relies on nationalism itself. Just as an individual needs boundaries of self and identified self-interests in order to enter into an interdependent relationship with another person, so any country must first secure its own boundaries, identity, and national needs and interests before it can have truly interdependent relations with other nations. Without such boundaries, a country is simply overrun. As Tony Wilden writes in *The Imaginary Canadian*: "The plain fact is that 'internationalism' refers to any relationship between two or more nations, each with control over its economy and its national territory. How then can such a term be applied to us, in any proper sense, when the country called Canada is not yet a nation?"[87]

To skip the stage of nationalism (which is also the stage of decolonization) and move into internationalism involves no real change in position as a colonized country. Rather, it magnifies the country's vulnerabilities to exploitation. Such an "interdependency" is little more than colonized dependency raised to the power of ten. It is also the effective silencing of a Canadian voice and identity, lost in an "internationalist" perspective.

In *The Bush Garden,* Northrop Frye considers the problem of national identity and, in one succinct passage, historically locates that problem for Canada:

> Cultural history, we said, has its own rhythms. It is possible that one of these rhythms is very like an organic rhythm: that there must be a period, of a certain magnitude, as Aristotle would say, in which a social imagination can take root and establish a tradition. American literature had this period, in the north-eastern part of the country, between the Revolution and the Civil War. Canada has never had it. English Canada was first a part of the wilderness, then a part of North America and the British Empire, then a part of the world.[88]

Although Frye uses cultural terminology, it is clear that he is referring to more than "culture" in the narrow sense of the term. The passage addresses a deeper *topos,* an imaginative position by which a people locate and identify themselves and thereby generate both culture and history. In those 1939 state-arranged public-relations events, Canada in pre–World War II years was being defined as "part of North America and the British Empire". During the war years, through both Mackenzie King's subservience to Anglo-American desires and Grierson's policy of "editorial internationalism", Canada was redefined as "a part of the world". But, as Frye implies, there is a necessary next phase in a country's development before making such a transition, a stage in which identity and place coalesce in the national imagination, or in Frye's words, the period "in which a social imagination can take root". For Canada, the significance of that missed phase makes the advocacy of internationalism a fully political choice on Grierson's part, and one that is a key to understanding his role in Canada.

Under hire to Great Britain's Imperial Relations Trust until mid-1941, and believing in the "boundary-crossings" necessary for "new economic integration", Grierson was unwilling or unable to recognize (or perhaps he fully intended) the political repercussions of his advocating an internationalist perspective for an already colonized country like Canada. If he perceived Canada during the war as "a new sort of place in the world", it was probably by comparison with a country like Mexico, which in 1938 had attempted to resist the wishes of the Big Three members of Beddington's Shell–Mex BP. Standing up to Standard Oil, Shell, and British Petroleum, Mexico's president Lazaro Cardenas nationalized the country's oil resources, thereby trying to resist the "new economic order" desired by the multinationals.[89]

As Grierson stated to his Canadian disciples, "We may forget nationalism but still need the cohesion and spur of national tradition."[90] If one significant aspect of Canada's "national tradition" was entrenched colonization by old and new empires, Grierson had already, years earlier, changed the connotation of the word "empire" to a more palatable-sounding and modernist expression. That "international combine of industrial, commercial, and scientific forces" was central to his wartime work in Canada.

5

Grierson and Hollywood's Canada

I hardly think that any one of us would wish to escape from the educational crusade to which we are called, in which the end is the internationalization of men's minds....

JOHN GRIERSON

Early in the war, Joseph Goebbels, the minister of popular enlightenment and propaganda for the Third Reich, made clear to his colleagues the "national morale-boosting" function of the cinema and the two significant roles, entertainment and education, that film could play in Hitler's "vital mission":

> Entertainment can occasionally have the purpose of supporting a nation in its struggle for existence, providing it with the edification, diversion and relaxation needed to see it through the drama of everyday life. But that is only its incidental purpose. By which I mean that today film has to serve a political function. It is a means of educating the people.[1]

Having taken over the German film industry, the Third Reich engaged in both feature filmmaking and newsreel propaganda, thereby meeting both political purposes. In line with Goebbels's recognition that "film is one of the most modern and far-reaching ways of influencing the masses today",[2] Fritz Hippler, state controller of German film, reiterated that cinema must focus on two needs of the public: "concentration and relaxation".[3]

Grierson had come to a remarkably similar view of the two purposes structuring the propagandistic use of film:

> We have our moods of resolution and also our moods of relaxation. The movies until now have concentrated on the moods of relaxation.... We have made a big business out of our moods of relaxation; we have not concentrated nearly so much on our moods of resolution. Yet, on the face of it, it is in our moods of resolution that we may be expected to build the future. These moods are worth organizing, just as deliberately as the movies, the newspapers and the show business generally, have been organizing our moods of relaxation.[4]

Viewing cinema from this perspective, as a way of deliberately organizing the moods of the public, Grierson was not about to tamper in Canada with that "big business" which had done such an effective and efficient job in the relaxation category. Indeed, during the war years, Hollywood would receive some useful assistance from Canada's film commissioner, while the NFB focussed on those "moods of resolution".

In later years, wartime NFB filmmaker Evelyn Spice Cherry stated the still predominant rationale: "Because our hands were tied in relation to the feature film industry, we would develop the documentary."[5] However, Canada's first film commissioner could have taken steps to untie those hands. Instead, he made the knots tighter.

By 1922 the Hollywood majors had formed their powerful lobby, the Motion Picture Association of America (MPAA). One of the first acts of the MPAA in its founding year was to set up a local bureau in Canada, called the Motion Picture Exhibitors and Distributors of Canada. Hollywood's vertical integration could successfully proceed only if those two aspects of the industry, distribution and exhibition, were well enough entrenched in Canada to prevent indigenous films from playing on local screens.

But it was also perceived to be a useful tactic, in the post–World War I milieu, for the Hollywood studios to make pictures about Canada. With Hollywood apparently serving the narrative needs of its neighbour, competition on the filmmaking front might be nipped in the bud. As film magnate Lewis Selznick expressed it at the time, "If Canadian stories are worthwhile making into films, American companies will be sent into Canada to make them."[6] Usually, though, it was cheaper for Hollywood crews to not even bother making the trip. In 1922 and 1923, the studio conglomerates made at least 65 feature films ostensibly set in Canada, with only a tiny minority actually filmed on location in this country.[7]

Besides being a way of eliminating competition from indigenous, small production companies, Hollywood's interest in constructing a screen image of Canada historically coincided with the larger pattern of branch-plant expansion north of the border in the 1920s. It was important to define Canada not only to its inhabitants but also to a U.S. populace engaged, if unwittingly, in the colonizing of its northern neighbour. The screen image of a Canadian hinterland, loosely populated by lumberjacks, Mounties, and mad Francophone trappers, conveyed an open territory in which U.S. industrial expansion would be unimpeded and perhaps even welcomed.

Throughout the 1920s, the MPAA clone, the Motion Picture Exhibitors and Distributors of Canada, wielded extensive lobbying power and influence in government and business circles. It became known as "The Cooper Organization", after its first president, Colonel John Cooper, who administered policies and practices with effective zeal.

In 1930, Colonel Cooper became a leading player for the opposition during the first legal challenge to Hollywood's hegemony in Canada. Indigenous film production had by that time been virtually snuffed out by the economics of the marketplace, and Canadian independent distributors and exhibitors were clearly next on the agenda. With Paramount's Famous Players subsidiary controlling virtually all first-run movie theatres in Canada, and with the Hollywood majors dominating film distribution, the local "indies" were being forced out of business all across the country. Their appeals to the government for action resulted in a combines investigation into the motion picture industry, launched by an order-in-council on September 23, 1930. Peter White was appointed commissioner of the investigation and asked to submit an interim report to the federal minister of labour.[8]

Despite intense lobbying by the MPAA and the Cooper Organization, Commissioner White was able to perceive the obvious.

> The Commissioner concluded that a combine existed in the motion picture industry within the meaning of the Combines Investigation Act, at least since 1926. He named all the U.S. distributors and also Regal Films Limited, which was a Canadian company, and Famous Players and some of its affiliates as parties to the combine. The Cooper Organization was also included in that list of companies.[9]

Commissioner White had set the stage in his interim report to the federal government for a dismantling of the American motion-picture cartel in Canada. Not only was the evidence patently obvious, but as film historian Peter Morris has noted, the "atmosphere was conducive to action", with the Canadian public disturbed by the predominance of American movies shown in Canada and offended by the inevitably distorted screen image of the country perpetrated in them.[10] A significant bandwagon of public opinion was rolling against the Hollywood majors and their control of the film marketplace in Canada.

But then there occurred one of those simple legal twists of fate that can upset even large-scale momentum.

> The government filed a suit under the Combines Investigation Act in 1932 against those offenders [but] in an Ontario court. How did a federal combines investigation end up as a provincial government suit in a provincial court? Apparently, there was some confusion as to who had the constitutional authority to administer justice in Canada.[11]

Film distribution was considered to be a matter of provincial authority, and the case against the American majors and the Cooper Organization was moved to what would be, for U.S. interests, easier and safer ground. The Hollywood industry had long been firmly entrenched in Ontario, with branch-plant distribution offices of the studio conglomerates located securely within the larger business community of the province.

The MPAA, through the lobbying efforts of Colonel Cooper, argued persuasively that the case before the Supreme Court of Ontario should be dropped.

> Among the statements attributed to the Colonel, when it was suggested that a 25 per cent quota be applied to Ontario theatres in favour of Canadian feature films, was this: 'The profits of the motion picture industry in Canada are in running theatres, not in the making and distributing of motion pictures.'[12]

Such a quota would have helped establish a precedent in Canada; at least one province would be taking protective and productive steps to foster indigenous filmmaking and ensure screen time for Canadian films. A decision against the U.S. cartel, even within a provincial court, would have been an historic turning point for the future of filmmaking in Canada.

> On March 18, 1932, Mr. Justice J. Garrow, in the Ontario Supreme Court, cleared the accused companies of all charges.... Famous Players [Paramount] and the American distributors were acquitted on the basis

> that the prosecution could not establish that the alleged combine was detrimental to the public interest as the ticket prices did not go up in the period under consideration.[13]

In 1939, U.S. control of film distribution and exhibition in Canada stood at virtual monopoly proportions, with 95 per cent of the box office and all first-run theatres in the hands of the studio conglomerates. Old Colonel Cooper was still fronting for the MPAA in Canada, and the state plan to establish a national film board was obviously not something that would slip past his attention. When the National Film Act was being debated in the House of Commons in the spring of 1939, Trade and Commerce Minister W.D. Euler hastened to assure his colleagues that the proposed NFB "would not enter into competition with private business".[14] Although on the surface this appears to have been an assurance to the small Canadian film production firms, like Associated Screen News of Montreal, Cinecraft Studios of Montreal, General Films Ltd. of Regina, Audio Pictures Ltd. of Toronto, Vancouver Motion Pictures, and Crawley Films of Ottawa, it was more obviously a reference to the Hollywood studio conglomerates, which would not countenance any infringement on their territory, whether in film production, distribution, or exhibition. Euler's assurances signalled the state's readiness to accept the existing cinema status quo.

Such assurances were no doubt greatly appreciated in the forthcoming months. The outbreak of World War II had an immediate effect on Hollywood's worldwide market. As Grierson wrote in 1940:

> I never saw so great a scurry in my life as in that first week of war in the chambers of Hollywood's magnates. A third of their world market had vanished overnight or become completely uncertain.... Hollywood was so nervous that it had a new idea every day. The first reaction was to draw in its economic horns, make cheaper pictures, intensify its American market. There was some talk of forgetting its international role and going all American. The result of that policy was seen in more pictures of North American history, more pictures of South America. Hollywood even began, in a sudden burst of light, to remember that Canada was a North American country.[15]

To both Grierson and those Hollywood magnates, "going all American" involved more than the continentalist connotation of the words, with even South America included in Hollywood's "domestic" mandate. Nevertheless, with its world market either vanished or uncertain, the Canadian box office of some $58 million annually was suddenly more precious to Hollywood than it had been in the prewar years.[16] Remembering that Canada "was a North American country", rather than merely a lucrative extension of the U.S. domestic box office, the MPAA, Hollywood's own foreign policy branch, was no doubt interested in whatever moves Canada's new film commissioner might make.

Colonel John Cooper had long been an effective lobbyist for MPAA interests by the time he encountered Grierson. If Cooper had anticipated any threat to Hollywood hegemony as a result of the film expert's appointment, it must have become quickly apparent to Cooper that the film commissioner had no intention of altering the status quo in Hollywood's Canada.

In 1940, Grierson's other assignment as film advisor for the Imperial Relations Trust sent him to Australia, where he was to organize a film propaganda base similar to the Film Board he had just gotten underway in Canada. If Colonel Cooper had any doubts about Grierson's views on Hollywood's "international role", those doubts were surely put to rest when Grierson recommended to the Canadian government that Cooper be invited to act as film commissioner during his absence.[17] The government readily complied.

According to Gary Evans, in recommending Cooper "Grierson was counting on Cooper's influence to prevent Famous Players from wrecking the young, fragile National Film Board and to keep commercial distribution of government films from being altered."[18] Grierson had made arrangements for the "Canada Carries On" series to be distributed by Famous Players and Columbia Pictures, thereby gaining access to virtually the entire theatre system owned or controlled by the Hollywood majors across Canada. But Grierson's recommendation of Cooper as interim film commissioner, and the government's compliance, can also be seen as an attempt to reassure the MPAA that Hollywood's territory would be left untouched and entirely intact, including that sizable box-office profit proceeding across the border throughout the war.

Quite early in his career, during his work for the Rockefeller Foundation and for Famous Players (Paramount), Grierson had recognized the significant role that Hollywood was playing in the formation of public opinion. In his later work for Stephen Tallents' Empire Marketing Board, he had also studied the vertically integrated international market that Hollywood maintained in Germany and France, and throughout Europe in general. Since at least 1927, then, Grierson had been familiar with Hollywood's economic monopoly in the realm of film and with various countries' attempts to alter that structure. Grierson's anti-nationalist politics for Canada, and his admiration of Hollywood's efficiency in managing the public's "moods of relaxation" resulted in important decisions beyond even the interim appointment of the MPAA's man-in-Canada, Colonel John Cooper.

Grierson was not about to infringe on Hollywood's territory in Canada, but he was not above a certain knowledgeable manipulation on the basis of potential nationalistic measures, if that manipulation suited his own interests. For example, in 1941 the NFB released the film *Warclouds in the Pacific,* an installment of the "Canada Carries On" series and an episode which gained distribution in the United States by United Artists. The film, another compilation production like most of the other films in the series, contained sequences from Louis de Rochemont's "March of Time" production outfit, which were provided with the understanding that any film incorporating the footage would be shown only in Canada.[19] When de Rochemont learned that the film was about to be distributed in the U.S. market, he began legal action to stop it. Gary Evans writes:

> According to Grierson, he and his counsel went to the Manhattan meeting of de Rochemont and the legal minions of Time-Life Incorporated with two legal weapons in their arsenal. First, his lawyer pointed out that the "March of Time" shots could be replaced by similar material from other stock-shot libraries. It would be easier not to tamper with the film and credit the "March of Time". The second weapon was a bald threat by Grierson. He claimed to have said, 'Gentlemen, I have it from the highest authorities in Canada that if the "March of Time" insists on pressing this suit, Canada will revise the existing laws regarding importation of foreign films to Canada.' A moment of silence followed, then one of de Rochemont's attorneys allegedly spoke. 'Louis, you started something you can't finish. Drop it.' No one was prepared to jeopardize the entire American film industry's open Canadian market over a few feet of film.[20]

When it came to an actual Canadian domestic-film policy, however, throughout his wartime tenure as film commissioner Grierson was firmly against both a film quota system and the revision of existing laws that left the Canadian market wide open. There is evidence that Grierson used his influential role to dissuade those "highest authorities in Canada" from taking any such legislated protectionist action.[21] His argument seems to have been that such moves would jeopardize the favoured-nation status that Canada had with the U.S. industry, though that "status" consisted of little more than the dubious honour of handing over the country's screens, industry, and box-office profits in exchange for U.S. distribution of Grierson's wartime documentary series.[22]

In the later years of the war, Colonel Cooper again had occasion to display his lobbying expertise on behalf of the MPAA, with no evidence of interference from Canada's film commissioner. As part of its effort to set price controls, the Wartime Prices and Trade Board attempted to set a ceiling on movie-ticket prices and film rentals, with a guarantee that theatre exhibitors would share films on a pro-rated basis. "This was the first structural policy intervention by the Canadian government since the aborted Combines law action of 1932," writes film historian Manjunath Pendakur.

> It was a direct blow to the American distributor's monopoly control ... because if the [Prices and Trade] Board were to succeed, the control of the market would shift from the American distributors to the Canadian government. Cooper and [J.J.] Fitzgibbons, the then-president of Famous Players, brought heavy lobby pressure on R.J. McMullen, the director of the Theatre and Film Section of the [Prices and Trade] Board, to stop him from altering the distribution market in any significant way.[23]

As a result, the U.S. monopoly structure remained firmly in place, and perhaps more significant, the Canadian government did not take what could have been the next important structural steps. Under wartime legislation, many of the jurisdictional realms of authority that had been the responsibility of provinces shifted to federal control. One of those jurisdictional shifts might have included responsibility for film distribution. But this provincial authority was left intact, to the benefit of the Hollywood majors. Similarly, the federal government, despite wartime financial needs, did not place a tax levy on Hollywood's box-office bonanza in Canada.

Throughout the war, Hollywood was able to count on its Canadian box-office market in the midst of uncertainty across the rest of its worldwide domain. But Commissioner Grierson also felt prompted to assist the U.S. studio conglomerates in their wartime production. While Canadian apprentices at the NFB were busy making films out of stock-shots, library footage, and pirated film sequences, Grierson was lining up film production work for U.S. companies in Hollywood.

According to Forsyth Hardy, in 1941 Grierson "flew to Hollywood where Stuart Legg met him and they lined up a dozen films to be made in co-production".[24] Peter Morris has discovered that Grierson's NFB was subsidizing the production of short films by Hollywood studios "'at a subsidy cost of approximately $1,000 a picture'".[25] These NFB–Hollywood coproductions were apparently meant to fill in gaps that the wartime NFB and Canada's private film companies were unable to meet. That, at least, is the most favourable interpretation of Grierson's arrangements with Hollywood during the war. According to Hardy, "In July 1941 he [Grierson] was on his way to Hollywood to arrange for Walt Disney to produce four films persuading Canadians to hold on to their War Savings Certificates."[26] Perhaps Grierson felt that Canadian filmmakers were not skilled enough for such a task.

Walt Disney's right-wing proclivities had begun to reveal themselves by at least 1939, when Leni Riefenstahl, "the leading propagandist for the Third Reich", visited Hollywood as Disney's guest.[27] According to Susan Sontag, four of the six films that Riefenstahl directed were documentaries "made for and financed by the Nazi government".[28] When Riefenstahl left Hollywood and returned to Germany in 1939, "she accompanied the invading Wehrmacht into Poland as a uniformed army war correspondent with her own camera team."[29] By a simple twist of fate, Grierson was also a friend of Riefenstahl, "from whose shoe he is said to have once drunk champagne at a party at the French Club in London".[30]

By 1940, Disney was adamant about keeping trade unionism out of his sizable studios. To prevent the Screen Cartoonists Guild from gaining a foothold, he formed a company union for his workers, in defiance of the terms of the 1935 Wagner Act.[31] Obviously, Mackenzie King's labour-relations solution for Rockefeller Junior was still popular among certain employers. The situation at the Disney Studios became increasingly untenable, and a strike was called on May 29, 1941, led by the Screen Cartoonists Guild.[32] With Disney refusing to negotiate with the union, the strike dragged on until August.[33] The dates of the strike indicate that Grierson's July 1941 visit to arrange four Disney–NFB coproductions occurred in the middle of the standoff. Apparently, not only did Grierson feel untroubled about using NFB funding to finance Hollywood coproductions, but he was quite willing to cross a picket line to do so.

Grierson's role as Canada's film commissioner throughout the war was, in an important sense, doubly compromised. Not only was he working for Great Britain's Imperial Relations Trust until mid-1941 to get a propaganda base underway for the Trust's interests in Canada and the United States, but he was actively working for the benefit of the Hollywood majors. It is not surprising, therefore, that when Grierson left the NFB and Canada in the autumn of 1945 one of the organizations that approached him for the possible employment of his services was the MPAA lobby, whose U.S. president, Eric Johnston, "was impressed by what he had achieved in Canada".[34]

All of these developments put Grierson's wartime achievements in a different light. The "prestige" series, besides training apprentices in an international viewpoint and employing a technique at the farthest remove from original shooting, were also a useful means for incorporating footage from Great Britain's Ministry of Information and constant references to England's wartime situation. Distributed across Canada and the United States, films in the "Canada Carries On" and "The World in Action" series thereby fulfilled Grierson's allegiances to the Imperial Relations Trust. But more important for Canada, the arrangement for commercial distribution of the series was apparently the tradeoff for leaving the Hollywood monopoly structure in Canada fully intact.

In this sense, the entire parallel structure of distribution and exhibition of NFB films for the non-theatrical circuits was another clear concession to Hollywood. Established in 1942, the non-theatrical circuits were an effective way of leaving the commercial box-office structure in place. As early as 1927, Grierson had conceived the idea of a "supplementary" distribution-exhibition plan which would not interfere with Hollywood's vertical integration. The NFB non-theatrical circuits instituted by Grierson during the war actually extended Hollywood's terrain while further marginalizing Canadian film. Though Grierson presented his non-theatrical circuits as a progressive and populist alternative, they might more realistically be seen as a way of maintaining the status quo in which Hollywood controlled virtually all of Canada's movie theatres and film distribution, thereby preventing indigenous production from gaining any more than a miniscule portion of screen time in Canadian theatres.

Grierson saw no reason for Canada to have a commercial film industry or to engage in its own feature-film production. In 1944, he recommended to the Canadian government that any such attempt in the postwar future would be too difficult, costly, counter-productive, time-consuming, and essentially unnecessary. For Grierson, the Canadian desire to make Canadian feature films was a sign of "old-fashioned nationalistic nonsense". Instead, the film commissioner outlined for the Canadian government his internationalist alternative:

> Are there not other possibilities for the development of Canadian film production? I think there are, and far more practical and possible than this dream of a Canadian Hollywood. One way is for Canada to make its feature films in New York or Hollywood. We might build up in either centre a company for the making of Canadian films with an associate producership in one of the big international companies.... Simpler still is the notion that the United States must increasingly appreciate its international obligations and give a quid pro quo for the benefits it receives abroad.... What can be asked of Hollywood, and is increasingly being asked, is that it should, as a matter of policy, spread its net wider for its themes.... I myself expect that before very long the big American companies trading in Canada will see to it that one or two films are devoted to Canada.... The next step, I expect, will be for Paramount to set aside a production unit in Hollywood for the production of Canadian feature films.[35]

No wonder the MPAA was interested in hiring Grierson after the war. As Peter Morris effectively argues, such a policy recommendation actually anticipated, and was undoubtedly the basis for, the infamous Canadian Co-operation Project of 1948, in which Hollywood agreed to insert dialogue references to Canada in U.S. feature films, in exchange for the Canadian government's agreement not to impose a quota system or tax on the domestic box office.[36] Grierson's 1944 "Film Policy for Canada" was circulated in Hollywood where it probably inspired the MPAA, which hatched the nearly decade-long Canadian Co-operation Project. In *Hollywood's Canada,* Pierre Berton discusses the project's public-relations role in promoting Canadian tourism and its silly inaccuracies about Canada. But Berton also identifies the real damage done by the project:

> From start to finish, the Canadian Co-operation Project was a public relations man's boondoggle. But from the point of view of the American film industry, it was remarkably effective. It prevented a quota system and thwarted any wistful hopes there might have been for a homegrown motion picture industry.[37]

The project also shaped the thinking of Canadian film policy-makers for years to come.

In his landmark article, "Backwards to the Future: John Grierson's Film Policy for Canada", published in 1986, Peter Morris argues convincingly that "John Grierson was a key architect of Canada's marginalization in the film world, and events and policies since his time simply part of a self-fulfilling prophecy."[38] However, Morris suggests that Grierson's "faith" in Hollywood and its international role was "derived from his often simplistic views on internationalism generally", that in relation to Hollywood, Grierson was "an innocent abroad".[39] Unfortunately, it's more complicated than that.

During the war, Grierson's independent Film Centre in London continued to be a viable concern, engaged in the production of public-relations films for industry and in bringing out the *Documentary News Letter,* for which Grierson wrote sporadically throughout the war and on whose editorial board he remained.[40] By 1944, the film scene in Great Britain was embroiled in a controversy surrounding U.S. domination of the British film industry, the role of independent British film producers in the face of the film combines, and a recommendation by Rank—owner of General Film Distributors, with links to Twentieth Century–Fox, United Artists, and Universal Pictures—that British producers adopt a particular strategy. That strategy was "based on Hollywood methods, which would involve producing expensive pictures designed for export and negotiating a share of the American market by exploiting links with the major American companies, using control of the British market as a bargaining counter".[41] An article in *Documentary News Letter* in 1944 summarized the mood of the time among British filmmakers: "The trouble is of course that the issues keep on getting confused. Everyone is agreed that we need a truly national film industry, and need equally a share in the world's screen time. The methods of achieving this, however, are the source of conflict. The danger of domination by the United States is clear enough."[42]

The dispute had obvious implications for government policy. Various pressure groups were formed to campaign for government intervention in the British film sector. One of the most active lobby groups was the British documentary movement, which canvassed for "radical measures" to be taken by the government.[43] Among those members advocating tougher measures in Great Britain for dealing with the Hollywood conglomerates was John Grierson, who was quietly working behind the scenes:

> In a private memorandum requested by the President of the Board of

> Trade in 1945, John Grierson and Paul Rotha, pioneers of the Documentary Movement, outlined a plan for a Government Film Corporation, which would have powers not only *to regulate the activities of private companies* but also to engage in production, distribution and possibly exhibition.[44]

In other words, at the same time that Grierson was advising the Canadian government not to intervene with Hollywood's screen monopoly in Canada, and not to foster a postwar Canadian film industry, he was actively engaged in the struggle in Great Britain for "a truly national film industry", calling for government regulation of Hollywood's private companies. Such discrepancies in his position throw a monkey wrench into the notion that Grierson in Canada was "an innocent abroad", but they also further confuse any clear understanding of his wartime politics and allegiances.

Adding to the confusion is the fact that Grierson, during the war, had also been advising the U.S. government on its film production.[45] In April 1945, leaks to the media revealed that Grierson was being considered to head up a film unit in the U.S. State Department to oversee its media needs.[46] Central to those needs was the expansion of American mass media worldwide, as officially announced in 1946 in the U.S. *Department of State Bulletin*:

> The State Department plans to do everything within its power along political or diplomatic lines to help break down the artificial barriers to the expansion of private American news agencies, magazines, motion pictures, and other media of communications throughout the world.... Freedom of the press—and freedom of exchange of information generally—is an integral part of our foreign policy.[47]

Hollywood and the MPAA lobby had long led the way, and provided the operative model, for such expansion. If the war had provided a temporary set-back to this planetary goal, the postwar milieu would more than make up for the delay in plans. Grierson's rhetoric to Canadian policy-makers about a "world of loyalty, faith and pride in which national barriers do not mean a thing"—the very rhetoric by which he convincingly persuaded the government not to foster an indigenous postwar film industry—was thus fully in line with the U.S. State Department's plans for the postwar future, plans that Grierson himself may have helped to influence.

Grierson had a poker in every media fire going at the time, so it's difficult to make sense of where he was coming from. Perhaps on some level, he was coming from "nowhere"—the "nowhere" that he encouraged his wartime Canadian apprentices to inhabit ideologically. But unfortunately, again it's more complicated than that.

One of the recipients of Grierson's expert media advice to the U.S. government during the war, whether directly or indirectly, was very likely Nelson Rockefeller, son of Junior, who as Assistant Secretary of State was (as of 1940) the co-ordinator of the Office of Inter-American Affairs (OIAA).[48] Having assembled a formidable staff of experts in the OIAA, Rockefeller intended to make the "Rockefeller shop" (as it was known) the centre of hemispheric diplomacy. The Publications and Information Division of the OIAA became the central thrust of the entire program and also "the first functioning propaganda agency in the [U.S.] government".[49]

Despite his government role, Rockefeller was also an executive for Standard Oil, which by 1941 had assumed a leading role in public opinion:

> The U.S. Legation at Managua, Nicaragua, reported that Standard Oil subsidiaries were distributing *Epoca,* a publication filled with pro-Nazi propaganda. John J. Muccio, of the U.S. Consulate, made an investigation and found that Standard was distributing this inflammatory publication all over the world. By a peculiar irony, Nelson Rockefeller was at that moment in his post of Coordinator of Inter-American Affairs, seeking to ensure the loyalty to United States interests of all of the governments of Latin America.[50]

Rockefeller, in his State Department role, was primarily concerned with a postwar hemispheric diplomacy that was anti-Communist. He strongly believed that the Nazis were a short-term problem in the hemisphere, but the Communists were an enemy that would remain to be dealt with long after Hitler had been vanquished.[51]

To consolidate U.S. interests in Latin America, Nelson Rockefeller sent Walt Disney (and, of course, Mickey Mouse) on a goodwill tour of South America in 1941.[52] The State Department financed the Disney entourage of nineteen and promised to underwrite each film made in South America up to $50,000.[53] As Grierson had observed during the first week of war, within "the chambers of Hollywood's magnates", the decision was made to go "all American" and "make more pictures of South America", a decision which nicely matched the plans of the State Department.

As the war proceeded, Nelson Rockefeller's efforts on behalf of hemispheric diplomacy revealed, despite the Soviet ally, an anti-Communist agenda central to the OIAA. Nicolo Tucci, head of the Bureau of Latin American Research in the State Department, resigned and called for the abolishing of the bureau.[54] "'My bureau,' he stated, 'was supposed to undo the Nazi and fascist propaganda in South America and Rockefeller was inviting the worst fascists and Nazis to Washington.'"[55] When Tucci took his complaints directly to Nelson Rockefeller, he was told, "'Everybody is useful and we're going to convert these people to friendliness to the United States.'"[56] Rockefeller knew that people like Stroessner, Somoza, and Trujillo could be relied on to be staunchly anti-Communist in the postwar years.[57]

As a threat to the workings of international business-as-usual, Communism remained throughout the war a continuing *bête noir* for multinational interests in Great Britain and the United States. Grierson, ever the skilled propagandist, made very few statements that clearly revealed a personal political stance, though many of his filmmaking colleagues in the British documentary movement in the 1930s at least felt themselves to be "'premature anti-fascists'" and socialists.[58] As Stuart Hood noted, "Politically, Grierson himself was more cautious, in spite of his radical-sounding phrases, and as his biographer, Forsyth Hardy, recalls, defined his position as being 'an inch to the left of whatever party is in office.'"[59] The vagueness of Grierson's internationalist rhetoric has prompted Gary Evans to write that Grierson "failed to see the shift of world economics toward monopoly capitalism".[60] There is little to support such a reading, considering Grierson's sponsorship formula throughout the 1930s, his work on behalf of Hollywood interests in Canada during the war, and his role as film advisor to the U.S. government. In his confidential report to the Canadian government in 1944, Grierson expressed this view:

> [Hollywood] is slowly learning that business can no longer operate in imperialistic terms, that it is no longer a question of getting yours and getting out, as it was in the nineteenth century with backward countries and backward peoples. *International business becomes progressively an international cooperative business*: not just a question of markets being exploited but of people's interest consulted and served. The American film business has been one of the last of the great international concerns to learn this, but it is learning.[61]

Whether in these terms Grierson was "an innocent abroad" remains to be seen.

6

Designs For Living and Dying

The present flow of social decency must lubricate the development of State planning, corporate thinking and co-operative [mass] citizenship.

JOHN GRIERSON, 1942

While Canadian film was being devoted to a seeming specialization in "moods of resolution" at the same time that Hollywood was further entrenching its hold on the industry, Canada's larger interests were being curtailed by the Allies meeting behind closed doors in 1942. Despite Canada's extraordinary contribution to the Allied effort, both Great Britain and the United States decided to reserve membership on various planning boards exclusively for themselves. The Combined Chiefs of Staff, the Munitions Assignment Board, the Combined Food Board, the Combined Shipping Adjustment Board, the Combined Raw Materials Board, the Combined Production and Resources Board "were composed exclusively of representatives of the British and United States governments".[1] Virtually all decisions about the war effort and planning for the postwar future were to be made by these two countries, with lesser Allies like Canada simply carrying out orders. As C.P. Stacey has written:

> It is an extraordinary fact that, although it is evident that it was expected that Canada's forces should be put at the disposal of the Combined Chiefs of Staff, and the lives of her soldiers, sailors and airmen hazarded in accordance with their decisions, the Canadian government never

received so much as an official notification that the Combined Chiefs of Staff had been set up. It got the information from the newspapers.[2]

The Canadian government's response to such outright marginalization and assigned subservience is revealing. Protests by the external affairs department led to the elaboration of what became known as the "Functional Principle", which J.L. Granatstein has termed "the one distinctive position that Canada produced during the war and almost a declaration of nationhood".[3] Drawn up in 1942, the Functional Principle argued that in specific fields Canada had legitimate claims to representation on boards planning for the present and the future. "In such 'functional' areas—the ability to produce food and raw materials, for example—Canada had world capacity and was, therefore, entitled to share in decision-making and responsibility."[4] This argument had some effect. Canada was finally allowed representation on the Combined Production and Resources Board and the Combined Food Board, but was given no say in areas deemed to be beyond its so-called "functional" capacities. Still being defined as essentially a base for international resource extraction, Canada was allowed no real voice in planning for the postwar future. Those plans were to reside in Anglo-American hands, whose competence was apparently beyond question.

According to the Functional Principle, world planning should depend on the co-ordination of "functions" through international co-operation, overseen by international institutions representing the interests of the countries concerned. As Gary Evans notes, "These were ideas that Film Board propaganda had already been emphasizing."[5] Whether Grierson was personally intervening in the thinking of the external affairs department is not known, but his influence with Mackenzie King was considerable.

Not surprisingly, one of Canada's assigned roles during the war was as a testing ground for chemical warfare weapons developed by British and U.S. scientists. In exchange for access to the research, the Canadian government willingly handed over a thousand square miles of land near Suffield, Alberta—as well as a number of Canadian servicemen—for the secret tests.[6] The British also used Australia, India, and Nigeria for similar chemical weapons tests throughout the war.[7] Clearly, it was useful for the two great powers to have such international co-operation from their colonized allies. Simultaneously, C.D. Howe's Department of Munitions and Supply was dutifully supplying the Manhattan Project with virtually all its uranium for the building of the atomic bomb.[8]

With the future being carved out for the benefit of certain Anglo-American interests, the war was obviously consolidating new alignments, particularly within what now would be called the military-industrial complex, but also across those national barriers that were such an impediment to "international co-operation".

As Grierson well recognized, film could provide people with useful guidance in complex times:

> Since it is a question of giving people a pattern of thought and feeling about highly complex and urgent events, we give it as well as we know, with a minimum of dawdling over how some poor darling happens to react to something or other. This is one time, we say, when history doesn't give a good goddam who is being the manly little fellow in adversity and is only concerned with the designs for living and dying that will actually and in fact shape the future.[9]

Convincing the public to accept those "designs for living and dying" that were shaping the future became central to Grierson's propagandist effort in Canada. Although the manufacture of consent had always been fundamental to his use of film, the war years called forth a particularly urgent insistence on his part. In what was undoubtedly his most controversial statement of the time, in 1941 Grierson admitted his "totalitarian" tendencies and expressed his belief that "you can be 'totalitarian' for evil and you can also be 'totalitarian' for good."[10] Grierson's statement expresses the questionable moral position that the end justifies the means, but it more obviously raises the question of just what Grierson considered the "good" to be.

At least a partial answer can be found in Grierson's view of the role of the people in the form of democracy he envisioned for the future. In 1942, he privately expressed his resolve: "Give me a year and I'll have taught progressive democracy to a nation as it hasn't been taught for a couple of generations."[11] His "progressive democracy" called for a new view of citizenship, a view similar to that of Walter Lippmann in the 1920s and Mackenzie King even before then. Grierson stated in 1941:

> What we are saying is that the belief in the voice of the people is wasteful and wrong only because it expects from the citizenry an impossible, because irrational, judgment. In other words, we are not throwing Democracy out, like the baby with the bathwater. What we are trying to arrive at is the point where we abandon that purely mystical concept of Democracy which encourages the illusion that ten million amateur

> thinkers talking themselves incompetently to death sound like the music of the spheres.... We do not want people to know everything about everything all the time, because it is impossible. We do not want them to make up their minds on specialized problems, because that is too much. We do not want to see them given, as individuals, a false notion of their freedom in society, and have them paralyze action with the infinite din of their amateur judgments.[12]

This passage, part of a speech delivered in Winnipeg in 1941, reveals that Grierson perceived his own audience—the very audience to which the NFB productions were addressed—as paralyzing action through their own "false" notions of freedom and democracy. Bristling with contempt for the millions of incompetent, irrational, "amateur" thinkers, the statement obviously suggests that Grierson was less interested in actually empowering people than in keeping them in their assigned place.

Contrasting his statement with one from a different political position underlines the limitations in Grierson's view. Throughout his life Frantz Fanon, Algerian political theorist and psychoanalyst, addressed questions of colonization and political struggle. He wrote: "Everything can be explained to the people, on the single condition that you really want them to understand. And if you think that you don't need them, and that on the contrary they may hinder the smooth running of the many limited liability companies whose aim is to make the people even poorer, then the problem is quite clear."[13]

Perhaps the key sentence in Grierson's statement is this one: "We do not want to see them given *as individuals,* a false notion of their freedom in society...." With his eye on the "co-operative or *mass* nature of society", Grierson was strongly against any individual deviation that might interfere with that "international combine of industrial, commercial, and scientific forces" on the horizon. In the Griersonian lexicon, individualism was as old-fashioned as nationalism for the modern age. Although Rockefeller Senior had preached a similar view for business—"The day of combination is here to stay. Individualism has gone, never to return"[14]—Grierson applied that perspective to citizenship and to democracy itself. "The false assumption," he wrote, "is the mystical democratic assumption that the citizen can be so taught to understand what is going on about him that he and his fellow in the mass can, through the electoral and parliamentary process, give educated and rational guidance to the conduct of the state."[15] Obviously, our incompetence, even "in the mass", stands in the way of "progressive democracy". But so does our notion of freedom:

> We know that much that has become precious to free men in a liberal regime must be forsworn in days of difficulty—the luxury of private possessions and private security—*the luxury of private deviation in thought and actions*—the supreme luxury of arguing the toss. Moreover, your individual trained in a liberal regime demands automatically that he be persuaded to his sacrifice. It may sound exasperating but he demands as of right—of human right—that he come in only of his own free will. All this points to the fact that instead of propaganda being less necessary in a democracy, it is more necessary.[16]

It would be reassuring to try to link such views to the temporary imposition of the War Measures Act in Canada and assume that, when the "days of difficulty" were over, Grierson would surely have seen such rights as more than "luxuries". But for Grierson the very notion of individualism was a remnant of nineteenth-century thinking, an "exasperating" refusal on the part of people to see themselves as part of a larger whole, the manageable mass required by technological and economic changes in the twentieth century. Because people were still "rotted in the old, untotal ways", propaganda was necessary to gain their consent.[17] In addition, it was also useful for the prevailing powers to implement "measures of authoritarianism which, the moment a country is driven to a common and total effort, prove completely logical and completely necessary".[18]

That "common and total effort" was not about to end with the war. As Grierson correctly perceived, there were "important shapes" on the postwar horizon: "The important shapes are obviously those more directly related to the national and international management of industrial, economic and human forces. They are important in winning the war without. They also represent, on a longer term view, a new way of thought which may be the deepest need of our generation."[19] Rather than resist our mass role in a fully mass society organized for the benefit of corporate multinational conglomerates, we have a deep "need" to give in to that consent so necessary for the orderly management of industrial, economic, and human forces. That management could in part be co-ordinated by the state:

> The State is the machinery by which the best interests of the people are secured. Since the needs of the State come first, understanding of these

> needs come first in education. If the operation of controls is necessary *for war or peace,* understanding of these controls is a necessary part of education.... Education has to give far more direct leadership and far less opportunity for the promiscuous exercise of mental and emotional interests.[20]

To Grierson, the public's emotional promiscuity seemed so deeply rooted that "it will certainly take continuous teaching of the public mind before the new relationship between the individual and the State, which total effort involves, becomes a familiar and automatic one."[21]

The war, however, was providing new opportunities for rational management:

> It is only my opinion, but it seems unlikely that the very dramatic and revolutionary centralization of financial, economic, and technocratic initiative in the State will be altogether undone after the war. We may, indeed, have given ourselves just that measure of social control which social justice and the complexity of the modern world demand, and on which there can be no substantial argument as between political parties.[22]

It is interesting that Grierson uses the term "revolutionary" in the context of a paragraph about "social control". The implication is that, for Grierson, "revolution" consisted of increasing mass allegiance to authoritarian power structures in order to ensure the better management of society. In this sense, it is important to consider precisely to whom the "ten million amateur thinkers" in wartime Canada were intended to relinquish their promiscuous mental habits. Obviously, "social control" was not something to be left to that exasperating "voice of the people", or even to the inefficiencies of parliamentary democracy. If Grierson was admittedly totalitarian, to what extent was his totalitarianism different from the other totalitarian ideologies competing for adherents in the first half of the twentieth century?

One way of exploring this question is to examine the portrait of the wartime enemy presented in the NFB documentaries. According to Gary Evans, whose book focusses on "the politics of wartime propaganda" at the NFB, most of the films concentrated on an "inspirational" message, with little or "no analysis of fascist ideology".[23] Evans writes that "Tom Daly, who learned his craft during these years and on these films, has explained that such analysis was not necessary since ... everyone knew what the Nazis were all about."[24] Nevertheless, there is a construct of the Nazi "enemy other" detectable in some of the films, and this construct serves as an interesting contrast and foil for the Griersonian political vision. The differences between Nazism and democracy as depicted in the films also offer a clearer insight into the differences between force and consent, those two "alternative sanctions" that Mackenzie King recognized as pertaining to all matters of law and government.

A comparison of the constructs of Nazism and democracy in the films exposes the taboo subjects which, though central to any real analysis of global geopolitics, the war, or the home front, were completely excluded from the wartime films. One of the taboo subjects was the plight of the Jews. With regard to this most heinous aspect of Nazism, there is simply a terrible absence in the films, mirroring Mackenzie King's Cabinet War Committee policy of remaining silent on "the Jewish question".[25]

Irving Abella and Harold Troper, in their book *None Is Too Many,* have documented the extent to which the Mackenzie King government was cognizant of the fate of the Jews under Hitler from the mid-1930s onwards.[26] But this dimension of the war, and of Nazism itself, was unmentionable in the NFB documentaries' geopolitical analysis. With access to captured German film footage, it is possible that Grierson viewed scenes of the persecution in the privacy of his screening room. Unfortunately, he seems not to have been asked about this aspect of captured enemy footage before he died. Whatever other reasons there were for this omission in the films' portrait of Nazism, one possible explanation is that, by leaving Nazism's racist and anti-Semitic basis unmentioned, it was thereby unnecessary to deal with a similar, if less virulent, racism within the democracies. The propaganda arm of the Canadian state could not mention this central aspect of Hitler's Reich without raising questions about Canada's own "well-defined pecking order of prejudice", to use James Gray's phrase. This subject was, however, only one of several taboos at work in Grierson's NFB films.

The most obvious comparison in the films is between two competing plans. *Tools of War* (1941) tells us, "It soon became clear that we were fighting more than men but a plan, a Giant Plan matured over six long years of labour." But democracy, too, had its own plan, one that had similarly matured over the years.

> Canada has her own plan, a plan gathering momentum and with its own roots down deep. Long before the war broke out, experts were quietly surveying Canada's industrial plants. Accurately they gauged the

> changes necessary for a shift to wartime production. This information has now become a master plan for total mobilization of Canadian industry.

On Guard For Thee (1940), one of the first compilation films made by the NFB, stresses the historical roots of this master plan:

> To the Department of Munitions and Supply falls the task of speeding up the organization of industry on an intensive war footing.... It's a task made easier by the industrial survey which the Defence Department undertook long before the threat of war, storing in its files detailed information on 2,000 plants.

It was the specific characteristics distinguishing these deeply rooted plans that became central to the films' construction of both ideologies.

As portrayed in various films, the most negative characteristic of the Nazi giant plan was its efficiency. *The Home Front* (1940) states, "Democracy faces the power of ruthless efficiency"; *Tools of War* claims that "Germany, with all its efficiency, began the devastation of Europe" and that it was an efficiency that was "regimented". As *Tools of War* explains, in Germany "people are ready and willing to accept regimentation", with their labour power taken from them "by decree". *Food—Weapon of Conquest* (1942) explains that German farmers were "under rigid orders of what crops to grow and in what quantity"; *The Labour Front* (1943) refers to the "robot ranks" of Germans and the "sweatshops where men labour for the greedy dreams of a chosen few". Thus, the Nazi giant plan is generally characterized as "ruthless", "efficient", "regimented" and operating by "decree". Moreover, it is a plan fully based on mechanization, with an "army forged in terms of twentieth-century mechanical science" (*Tools of War*). Virtually all film references to German battle and strategy stress the mechanization behind Nazi power. Since the films could not refer to Nazi racial policy, these characteristics become the general parameters of the ideology of the enemy.

To distinguish it from the giant plan of Nazism, the master plan of democracy could not be associated with ruthless efficiency, regimentation, mechanization, or operation by decree. This posed a difficult challenge to the powers of rhetoric, given the real conditions at work at the time. So, for example, *Tools of War* states:

> Parliament passed an Emergency Defence Act giving the State control over every national asset: manpower and wealth alike.... To counter

> regimented Nazi efficiency, democracy under stress of war demanded and got the planned and total effort of a free people.... The old tradition of muddling through vanished to be replaced by a plan: the complete mobilization of civilians and soldiers, men and women, factory hands, farmers, and office workers. For the first time in history, nations now clashed in a war of organization. And against the slave economy of the Nazis stood the planned and united effort of democracy in arms.

The demands of the state, along with the passage of an Emergency Defence Act, are apparently different from operating "by decree". Similarly, "regimented efficiency" seems to be different from "planned and total effort". German farmers are under "rigid orders" to grow certain crops and quantities, but this appears not to be the same as the "planned abundance" (*Thought For Food,* 1943), a campaign by which Canadian farmers were encouraged by scientists to shift from wheat production to growing rye, oats, and barley for the war effort. Whereas German labour has been regimented into a "slave economy", "the workers of Canada have placed national interest above everything" (*Labour Looks Ahead,* 1945). According to *The Labour Front,* "Gone perhaps forever is the old haphazard system of employment. Instead, for every man who wants it, there is training to fit his personal skill to the needs of war production." Similarly, the Canadian farmer is to be "integrated into a new way of life by total war", an integration based on "a vision of well-ordered citizenship" (*Battle of the Harvests,* 1942).

A democratic master plan based on "order", "planning", and "united" and total effort, "state control over every national asset: man-power and wealth alike" indicates a new degree of centralized power that would alter every "old haphazard system". As *Tools of War* states:

> No longer does unchecked competition impair the nation's efficiency. For this group of civil servants, businessmen and technical experts controls all Canada's natural resources and manufacturing plants in the public interest. They can tell producers what to make and when to deliver. They can even take over factories and schedule their productions.

Although Nazi efficiency is to be despised, the control and efficiency resulting from "expert" planners is to be marvelled at and accepted without question.

One of the obsessions running throughout the wartime documentaries is the central importance of the scientific expert, especially in "mechanized war". According to *The Battle of Brains* (1942), "This war is a conflict of strategy and organization, of technical apparatus, of science, mechanics and morale".

> Behind all the busy activity of the factories, working unobtrusively but ceaselessly ... stands the Canadian scientist. First in line in the national chain of laboratories is the National Research Council. Here, as in the laboratories run by universities and manufacturing firms and public bodies all over the country, the scientist takes his place beside the military scientist as a devisor of victory.

It is the expertise of science that is "helping to take the gamble out of farming" (*New Plans for the Land,* 1943) and provide "a program of scientific diet" (*Thought for Food,* 1943) for the nation. It is "scientific training and scientific feeding" (*Battle of the Harvests,* 1942) that is necessary for both a military victory and "a new Canada built on foresight and cooperation". In "the technician's warfare of today", it is the combination of "scientist and soldier" that will lead to a "new efficiency" in military life (*Letter From Aldershot,* 1940). The ideal of this scientist-soldier is best represented by Lieutenant General A.G.L. McNaughton, who appears several times in the wartime documentaries. Much is made of him, for example, in *The Battle of Brains*:

> It is no accident that the former chief of Canada's National Research Council, Lieutenant-General McNaughton, is now commander of her armies overseas.... More than anything else, this brings home to Canadians that in this war the soldier and the scientist are united.... Behind all the urgency of Canada's effort is the quiet work of the men of the laboratories, always ready ... to devise new weapons for the future. And Canada knows that as long as this link is maintained between the soldier and the scientist, she will be ready for any new methods of warfare.

For many Canadian viewers the choice of McNaughton as the films' representative soldier-scientist may have had another resonance. During the 1930s, McNaughton had served as administrator for Canada's Unemployment Relief Camps, a relief program run by the Department of National Defence to take care of the problem of single unemployed men.

> The official rationale for this plan was that problems of declining morale and health made transient men easy prey to Communism. To prevent this fate, the unemployed men's independence and initiative had to be restored by useful work and discipline.[27]

The state had itself caused the problem of transience by setting regulations by which teenagers reaching the age of 18 were cut off from family-relief benefits. Forced to go on single relief, "which meant eating at soup-kitchens and sleeping in slum-area rooming houses", the single unemployed throughout the Dirty Thirties usually joined the cross-country search for work.[28] The camps set up by the Bennett government had less to do with restoring independence and initiative than with ensuring that the Communist menace would be contained.

> No organization of any kind was permitted in any camp, and no petition could be circulated, and no committee could be formed to complain about anything. Anyone with a grievance could take it to the foreman of his gang, then appeal to the foreman of the sub-camp or the supervisor of the project. But he could do it only by himself without the vocal or moral support of a comrade. Anyone who tried to organize a protest in a camp faced expulsion and in some camps that meant being expelled in midwinter at the camp gates a hundred miles from the nearest habitation.[29]

During the war, these same camps housed some of the 25,000 POWs sent to Canada by Great Britain, the 22,000 Japanese-Canadians rounded up by the Mackenzie King government, and more than 2,000 of the 30,000 refugees from Germany and Austria arrested by Great Britain in 1940 as "enemy aliens". Sent to Canada for confinement during the war, these refugees were primarily Jews, trade unionists, and socialists escaping from Hitler's purge, only to meet in Great Britain measures of "security" that forcibly removed them from the continent.[30] Mackenzie King, busy arresting his own "suspect" citizenry, was willing to oblige Great Britain's penal needs.

If the figure of McNaughton is used in the films as a representative of the soldier-scientist ideal, the equation should include the efficient administrator, during the Dirty Thirties, of anti-Communist measures for the masses. Soldier-scientist-camp administrator would find its most efficient and horrible expression in Germany, but it is possible to find less heinous examples unfolding in democracy at the same time. As *On Guard For Thee* explicitly states, "As the first year of the war runs out, to Canada comes the realization that Hitler must be beaten by his own methods."

The adoption of the enemy's methods makes it somewhat difficult to distinguish between competing ideologies. Ann Gomer Sunahara has written of the internment of Japanese-Canadians:

> While certainly less extreme than those practised by the Third Reich, the actions of the Canadian government were nonetheless also based on the

> political exploitation of racism, and in the Canadian case, such tactics were cruelly hypocritical. The Canadian government betrayed not only Japanese Canadians but also the men and women it was sending to Europe and Asia, making a mockery of the principles for which they were fighting and dying.[31]

But this contradiction is central to understanding the kind of democracy that was being constructed under the aegis of war. The giant plan of Nazism and the master plan of democracy tended to coincide and overlap in certain areas. *This Is Blitz* (1942) claims that, under the guidance of "military experts and scientists the world over", democracy was building "a war machine beyond the wildest dreams of the Nazis", a claim that exposed similar dreams behind both ideologies.

Intent on "the obliteration of economic anarchy and disorder all over the world",[32] Grierson believed that a technocracy of scientific and business experts could create order and efficiency through "the national and international management of industrial, economic and human forces".[33] For all his advocacy of state initiative and co-ordination, however, Grierson did not perceive this state endeavour in socialist terms. In 1941 he wrote:

> My point is that in maintaining so stubbornly the old individualist, sectional, free competitive and nationalist viewpoint, we have been holding to concepts which may have, in their day, been great and glorious concepts capable of motivating men to great achievements, but which are incapable of mastering the problems of today. I regard it as foolish and unnecessary to say that financial industrial forces have been selfish or that labour has been blind.... To make my argument still clearer, let me say that I am not talking of the passage from Capitalism to Socialism ... I do not believe that Socialism as we have thought of it will come at all.[34]

Socialism was not on the horizon of Grierson's political vision for the future, but a new stage of international capitalism, managed by an expert technocracy, was.

In his wartime speeches and writings, Grierson seldom addressed directly the issues surrounding technological innovation in the first half of the century. It could be argued, though, that technology is the subtext of his rhetoric, that it is implicit within phrases like "the complexity of the modern world", "mastering the problems of today", and "the management of industrial, economic and human forces". In 1941 he wrote: "We have loosed the inventions and armed the human race with brilliant physical weapons for creating a rich civilization. But we have not known how to solve the simplest problems of economic integration either nationally or internationally."[35] For Grierson, technological development and international economic integration seem inextricably linked, with the move towards a technocracy of expert planning facilitating economic integration and multinational corporate expansion.

Grierson found a focus for scientific and expert management in the massive, efficient factories turning out war material at a spectacular rate of production, 24 hours per day, seven days a week. Long after the war, Margaret Ann Adamson (Elton), one of the NFB filmmakers who worked for Grierson, recalled: "Grierson always regretted his own inability to easily understand science and technology, and it may not be unfair to say that the 'aesthetics of technology' never took root in Canada."[36] On the contrary, the wartime NFB documentaries are steeped in precisely this aesthetic, with lengthy and numerous sequences shot in the huge munitions factories of the Allied nations, panoramic long-shots within the vast factories of Canada, the United States, and Great Britain turning out planes and tanks, extensive tracking shots through the assembly-lines of war production, impressive batteries of tractors and farm machinery bringing in the crops. That technological fetish detectable in Grierson's films of the 1930s blossomed during the war into a celebration of machine efficiency and technological prowess.

As *The Labour Front* states, this war is "the struggle of machines", and in the representation of that struggle on film, technology dwarfs the human being. Over long-shots of the vast factory enclosures, *Industrial Workers of Central Canada* states that "inside the plants, man seems almost a stranger." The visuals drive home this machine supremacy, with technology foregrounded in the frame while the small and anonymous human beings toil on the line. It is the building of this great machine that the wartime films seem to celebrate: not just the "sleek metal monsters of incredible speed and power" (*On Guard For Thee*) being turned out on the assembly-lines, but the building of a new society entirely modelled on the machine. "From the start, Canada has realized the importance of mechanization," *The Battle of Brains* claims, and it is that mechanization which is an underlying principle of Grierson's vision for "progressive democracy".

The assembly-line becomes the central figure in this aesthetic of technology. *Tools of War* celebrates this "new world of mechanical precision" and, bypassing the labour of the human beings, enthuses over the fact that, to make each Bren gun, "18,000 tools and jigs must have done their work to the accuracy of a split hair—18,000!" As the camera tracks through the vast plant, the voice-over explains: "In the cause of national efficiency, private competition is ended, all blueprints are standardized, all parts interchangeable." This standardization and interchangeability of parts mirror the army ideal; and in *Battle Is Our Business* (1943) a Canadian private claims (in one of the few uses of sync sound): "We learn to do things together and at the same time." Such co-ordinated precision is the central theme of *Industrial Workers of Central Canada,* which relies on panoramic shots inside huge factories where "modern industrial workers are specialists ... the workers perform one operation over and over on the assembly-line. Even so, "machines do a great deal of the work".

War primarily benefits industry and corporate power, and in the case of World War II, the emergency of wartime provided a useful occasion for expanding and fully retooling factories, for replacing human workers with automation. With skilled labour recruited for the military, industry could justify expanded automation and further stratification and subdivision of the production lines as being necessary for both increased production and the hiring of non-skilled labour, especially women who could be quickly laid off after the war. Analyzing this aspect of Canadian wartime industry, Ruth Roach Pierson writes: "Impressed by 'scientific management schemes' developed in Britain and the U.S., the Inter-Departmental Committee on Labour Co-ordination recommended in December 1941 that, to reduce the demand for skilled labour, 'jobs will be broken down....'"[37] Governmental co-operation with the needs of industry increased job alienation, creating even more monotonous line-work than before; it increased as well the vulnerability of the workers' status. As Pierson argues, the minimal training necessary for this stratified work meant that non-skilled labour was dispensable, and such routine tasks on the line could be turned over to a machine.

The wartime documentaries tend to hail such technological advances as examples of modern efficiency and planning. *The Strategy of Metals* (1941) includes several sequences that are nothing less than an impressive hommage to mechanization, a kind of *ballet méchanique* in which the roar and screams of industrial machines on the sound track accompany the fascinating montage of sparks flying, pistons and parts moving, great pieces of equipment and machines all rhythmically syncopated. In *Smoke and Steel* (1943) a "nation's will to produce" is reflected in a huge factory said to employ some 30,000 workers, described as "men who have grown up with the assembly line".

Quietly tending the great machine, this anonymous mass is smoothly co-ordinated to the pace of the line as the camera surveys this panorama of efficient production.

This anonymous mass must be efficiently housed in order to work productively, and *Wartime Housing* (1943) features the prefabricated houses turned out by a Crown corporation, Wartime Housing Ltd., with "all the precision of assembly-line technique". The houses were erected in 36 hours and came in four standardized styles. Instead of an "evil rash of tarpaper shacks", the film states, there are "neat rows of H-12s and H-22s". Most significant, however, "it is possible to pull down the houses when the needs of industry shift." The needs of corporate industry, like the needs of the state itself, must come before the everyday domestic needs of people. In an important sense, these wartime films continually stress the necessity for the standardization of both worker and daily life in order to fit the needs of the machine. Regardless of how often the films might enthuse about "the people's century", the "din of their amateur judgments" is meant to be drowned out by the scream of the machine and silenced by the cool rationale and orderly planning of the expert scientific technocrats, whose master plan is to proceed without question. A line from *Corvette Port Arthur* (1943) captures the desired efficiency of state: "The convoys sail on, having no choice and wishing no other." Grierson's vision of democracy for the future was thus fully in line with, as he put it, "the designs for living and dying that will actually and in fact shape the future".

Although Grierson claimed on at least one occasion that he found such assembly-line sequences boring, they were nevertheless an intrinsic part of his ideological vision and had been since the 1930s. Of the British documentary movement, he said: "We put glistening patterns of vigour and skill and mass industrial achievement against the sky and men today accept them as part and parcel of the testament of beauty. We did so because governments wished to celebrate the essential terms of modern citizenship and because industrial corporations wished to celebrate their public utility."[38] Grierson's documentary movement was neither an interrogation of nor a challenge to the mainstream views of the time. Rather, documentary under Grierson was in service to those powers of the status quo that were bringing about a "mass industrial achievement" apparently beyond question. As at least one film scholar has noted, although other independent documentary movements of the 1930s were taking an anti-fascist stance on the turn of geopolitical events, Grierson's British documentary movement endorsed a "system of 'general consent'" to the larger forces at work in society.[39]

"We are seeking," Grierson wrote in 1941, "a method of articulating society which will communicate a sense of the corporate and a sense of growth.... [Documentary] does not teach the new world by analysing it. Uniquely and for the first time it communicates the new world by showing it in its corporate and living nature."[40] As the predominant figure in the ethos of the new world, the assembly-line spoke volumes about industrial growth and corporate management. Questions of ownership of the means of mass production and of the benefits to be gained in the corporate sector through such growth were apparently beyond documentary analysis. For Grierson, it was enough to communicate the modern world, not interrogate it, through a "testament of beauty".

Beneath the oppositional, semantic rhetoric of the wartime films' voice-overs, it is difficult to determine just where the filmic constructions of the Nazi giant plan and the democratic master plan differ from one another. Both plans seem to be characterized by the values of mechanization, standardization, efficiency, a degree of regimentation, and social control by an élite. Since the films are silent on Nazi racial policy and the extermination of so-called "non-productive" elements in the Third Reich, the burden of ideological difference resides in the opposition between nationalism and internationalism, between force and consent in propagandist terms, and in a crucial distinction between emotion and reason.

Battle Is Their Birthright (1943) speaks of the "young fanatics of the Third Reich" over shots of German boys singing together, exercising together. *Tools of War* mentions "the doctrine of strength through joy" with shots of Hitler Youth enjoying their outing in the countryside. *Food: Weapon of Conquest* refers to the "mystic Nazi doctrine of blood and soil", while *The War For Men's Minds* (1943) includes shots of Nazi officers drinking wine and drunkenly toasting one another as the voice-over refers to "the philosophy of despair". This emotional element in Nazism is important to understanding Grierson's oppositional "totalitarianism". At the top of his list of those industrial, economic and human forces in need of management by scientific experts was the human psyche.

7

The Pursuit of Sacrifice

Given the conditions of modern technocracy, workers' self-management represents an unpractical and inefficient [ideal]. My view, if any, would be that we are entering upon a new and interim society which is neither capitalist nor socialist, but in which we can achieve central planning without loss of individual initiative, by the mere process of absorbing initiative in the function of planning.

JOHN GRIERSON, 1941

Part of the problem in differentiating the warring ideologies as depicted on film lies in modernist technocracy itself, which did in fact provide the common basis for what the NFB films called the enemy Giant Plan and the democratic Master Plan. Underneath the competing ideologies there was a shared enthusiasm for the goal of full mechanization. As the predominant ethos of the century, technological efficiency provided the common link, though Great Britain and the United States had long been in the lead on this front. As Siegfried Giedion writes in *Mechanization Takes Command*:

> The assembly line and scientific management are essentially rationalizing measures. Tendencies in this direction extend relatively far back. But it was in the twentieth century that they were elaborated and became a sweeping influence. In the second decade (with Frederick Taylor as the central figure), it was scientific management that aroused the greatest attention: the interest of industry, the opposition of workers, public discussion, and governmental enquiries. This is the period of its further refinement and of its joining with experimental psychology (Frank B. Gilbreth, central and most universal figure). In the third decade (Henry Ford, the central figure), the assembly line moves to the key position in

> all industry.... In the time of full mechanization, the production engineer gained sway over manufactures of the most diverse types, seeking every possible opening in which an assembly line might be inserted.[1]

These "rationalizing measures" for industry were a logical outgrowth of the Enlightenment which had long served to raise Reason to the dominant position in the Western psyche.

To an extent, German Romanticism was a reaction to this trend in Western thought with its split between reason and emotion, logos and eros. The Germanic movements and philosophies of the turn of the century were based on a rejection of the supremacy of reason, with its seemingly sterile forms of abstraction considered anathema to the heirs of the Romantic movement. In contrast to the dominant values of rational analysis and scientific abstraction, emerging German ideology in the post–World War I years was looking to its past to uncover lost values of soul, feeling, concrete immediacy, and experience—values which were (perhaps not ironically under patriarchy) to be found primarily in men's experience at the battlefront. Nostalgia for the immediacy of battle, as well as for a time preceding the humiliation Germany felt under the Treaty of Versailles, was intermixed with resentment towards those perceived to have benefitted from Germany's defeat.

While Germany's nationalism was looking backwards, past modernity, to a more Romantic era, the political leadership was nevertheless simultaneously embracing modernity's fundamental focus: modern invention and modern technology. It is in this sense that Jeffrey Herf writes of the Weimar and Third Reich politics and culture as outgrowths of "reactionary modernism": an incorporation of the modernist technological project into reactionary politics which glorified past ages and lost values.[2] Hitler's well-known admiration for Henry Ford was based not only on Ford's virulent anti-Semitic writings, but also on the U.S. industrialist's genius in production.[3]

By 1938, Charles Bedaux—who in the 1920s and early 1930s had introduced brutal methods of production based on time-motion studies and assembly-line speed-ups to plants run by ITT, Standard Oil, General Motors, and Ford—was appointed head of I.G. Farben's commercial operations under the Third Reich.[4] Clearly, those modern "rationalizing measures" of production could also be reconciled with reactionary politics.

Herf quotes from a speech Joseph Goebbels made in 1939 to open the Berlin Auto Show:

> We live in an era of technology. The racing tempo of our century affects all areas of our life. There is scarcely an endeavour that can escape its powerful influence. Therefore, the danger unquestionably arises that modern technology will make men soulless. National Socialism never rejected or struggled against technology. Rather, one of its main tasks was to consciously affirm it, to fill it inwardly with soul, to discipline it and to place it in the service of our people and their cultural level. National Socialist public statements used to refer to the steely romanticism of our century. Today this phrase has attained its full meaning. We live in an age that is both romantic and steel-like, that has not lost its depth of feeling. On the contrary, it has discovered a new romanticism in the results of modern inventions and technology.... National Socialism understood how to take the soulless framework of technology and fill it with the rhythm and hot impulses of our time.[5]

Goebbels's "steely romanticism" was an apt term for Nazism's reconciliation of German Romanticism with modern technology, but not with modernity itself because of modernity's loss of soul.

It can be argued that both Nazism and the Western democracies were, each in its own way, seizing the "soulless framework of technology" and filling it with different conscious and unconscious projections. Although the scientific pragmatism and positivism of the Western Allies may appear to be a denial of "the steely romanticism of our century", nonetheless, the fascination and faith in the potentials of science and full mechanization bespoke an underlying romance with technology in the democratic project as well.[6]

Grierson fully shared that optimism about technology so characteristic of his time, but he was concerned as a propagandist to distinguish it from the soulful and romantic views on technology held by Goebbels and the Nazis. At the same time, however, Grierson was faced with the urgency of convincing Canada to undergo a rapid industrial transformation that would otherwise have taken half a century or more. This challenge—to propagandize the necessity for technological innovation without endorsing "steely romanticism"—provides a tension in the wartime NFB films and within Grierson's own totalitarian politics.

Peter Morris has revealed at least one aspect of that mystifying organization, the Imperial Relations Trust, to which Grierson was under contract until mid-1941:

> It is generally well-known that in Britain before the war there were many

> people in positions of power who favoured British accommodation with Germany, if not full collaboration. When Churchill became Prime Minister none of these people were prosecuted. They were simply moved to less sensitive positions. Among them were some members of the Board of the Imperial Relations Trust for whom Grierson was working on contract. I do not know whether there is any direct evidence that Grierson was suspected of being a collaborationist. But his views on the state and on the alleged weaknesses of liberal democracy were well known.[7]

Whatever Grierson's political allegiances were at the time, it is clear from his writings and the wartime films made under his tutelage that his totalitarian vision was purposely anti-Romantic. His overriding concern for order was in obvious contrast to Goebbels's "hot impulses of our time" or "depth of feeling". Although Grierson and the Western democracies had embraced technology at least as fully as did the Third Reich, and with as much enthusiasm, there was a need to maintain the semblance of a coolly rational approach to full mechanization by the heirs of the Enlightenment.

This difference seems important to understanding Grierson's politics and to differentiating between the Nazi giant plan and the democratic master plan as constructed in the wartime NFB films. Although beneath the semantic rhetoric both plans tend to be characterized as valuing mechanization, standardization, efficiency, some degree of regimentation, and social control by an élite, it is in the arena of disciplined technological advancement that the two plans differed.

After June 1941, with Germany's invasion of the Soviet Union, both Great Britain and the Soviet Union were in a desperate struggle for their existence. With the entry of the United States into the war after Pearl Harbor, the U.S.-British-Soviet alliance was temporarily solidified, although, as Bertram Gross notes, "The coalition was not an alliance against fascism as such."[8]

The key weakness of the Third Reich, despite its embrace of a "steely romanticism", was that compared to the United States the Nazis were "technologically backward".[9] Though they did not lack for good scientists and physicists, the Nazis did not have "a mature technostructure closely linked with top political and military leadership".[10] By contrast the Allied nations had long been building such a technostructure, and one firmly based in scientific rationalism. During the war, it quickly matured into the "military-industrial complex", which was not about to be dismantled after World War II. The wartime NFB films made under Grierson's tutelage continually underline this difference. For Grierson, the international dimensions of that technostructure were of primary concern, expressed in his belief in the necessity of economic border-crossings and "Empire integrations".[11]

Within Canada, C.D. Howe's Department of Munitions and Supply provided the model for the efficient operation of a technostructure co-ordinated by state and corporate initiative. In 1941, Grierson wrote:

> Vast changes in the structure of the State have been wrought during the war and particularly since April 1940 [the date on which Howe's department was established]. Before the war we lived in what was brightly called a free society. Freedom of contract, freedom of production, freedom of investment, freedom of choice, freedom of prices and freedom of the devil to take the hindmost.... By and large the dream of a free society still held. When one thinks of the speed with which we discarded this dream, and how prepared and ready our statesmen and specialists were to discard it, we are bound to conclude that the desire for discipline and total effort, and the willingness to accept price, profit, age and other controls were there all the time, and not only for war but also for peace.[12]

Full consent to those controls established by "specialists" would also have to include the elimination of old, "untotal" emotional patterns:

> We shall talk less about free enterprise and competition and more about the State as a partner in initiative. There will be less about Liberty and more about Duties: less about the pursuit of Happiness and more about the pursuit of Sacrifice. Above all, there will be less about words and more about action and less about the past and more about the future. Already you hear the new words in the air: Discipline, Unity, Co-ordination, Total Effort, Planning. They are the first swallows over the horizon; and there are going to be more of them.[13]

Just as the "promiscuous exercise of mental and emotional interests" must be discouraged, so too liberty and the pursuit of happiness must give way to duties and the pursuit of sacrifice. Such a society would be characterized by a high degree of production. As one wartime NFB filmmaker observed, "One might analyze the hundreds of films with which Grierson was associated, and demonstrate that their images were all about *work*...."[14] As Gary Evans indicates, the wartime NFB made only two films about sport and leisure, *Hot Ice* and *Ski in the Valley of the*

Saints.[15] Grierson's emphasis on duty and sacrifice became an obsession in the films with production and labour for total effort. Yet Peter Morris observed:

> Although Grierson speaks of a "documentary of work and workers", it is clear he is only speaking of *some* work and *some* workers. Indeed, the list of those not included seems more remarkable in retrospect than those who were included. I give just one example: absent is any depiction of the group of workers to which Grierson himself belonged—the technocrat in government.[16]

There is one film, *Ottawa: Wartime Capital* (1940-41), that does focus on the "17,000 civil servants and industrial experts" who have transformed the "quiet city known to tourists" into a bustling scene of technocratic efficiency. But rather than examining their actual role, the film seems more intent on impressing the viewer with the vastness of the secretarial pools, the extensiveness of record-keeping and filing, and scenes of orderly (if unexplained) meetings of officials and civil servants. The scenes devoted to governmental workings seem particularly mystifying. The War Measures Act is termed "the swifter process of Cabinet decision". Scenes of mail censorship are passed over without comment. And one particular image lingers in the mind: inside the Parliament buildings, the House is in session. As the camera rolls, the great wooden doors swing closed to the viewer, blocking any view of governmental procedure. The message is clear: the workings of Parliament itself are apparently beyond the comprehension of our "amateur" thinking.

The strong tendency in the films, and in Grierson's totalitarianism, is the underlining of an unquestioning and automatic subservience to authority, abandoning liberty for duty, sacrifice, work, discipline, co-ordination, planning. But how can such a view be distinguished from the mobilizing views Hitler held? In a speech, the Fuhrer said: "National Socialism is not a doctrine of inertia but a doctrine of conflict. Not a doctrine of happiness or good luck, but a doctrine of work and a doctrine of struggle, and thus also a doctrine of sacrifice."[17] It is precisely in Hitler's words "conflict" and "struggle" that the difference is to be found, as well as in the nature of the sacrifice Grierson had in mind.

Peter Morris, continuing his analysis of the ideology of the wartime documentaries, writes:

> The image is almost always of workers *working*. This has sometimes been discussed in terms of the depiction of the dignity of labour. But one wonders why there are so few images of workers in their domestic or private lives. Or, indeed, of workers at leisure, workers playing. It's possible to think here of the contrast with some of Humphrey Jennings' films such as *Spare Time* or *Listen to Britain* which do, in fact, show workers in other contexts than factories.[18]

But play and leisure have nothing to do with duty and sacrifice, and they tend to allow for certain anarchic-emotional impulses that threaten to go beyond the control of technocratic authority. In perhaps his most strict pronouncement about the future, Grierson wrote in 1942: "we are entering an era of action, in which only the givers of order and the doers generally will be permitted to survive."[19] Not just profit, but survive. Uncontrolled play and unmanaged leisure are a threat to the "givers of order". Both may subvert all the values posited by Grierson, as well as in their essence be perceived as part of the (twisted and perverted) pseudo-Dionysian vein in Nazism. Play is non-productive, inefficient, emotional, and individualist—the shadow side of all that Grierson upheld as central to scientific planning. Like emotion itself, play may appear to verge on chaos, especially the seeming chaos of the unconscious which gives rise to personal and collective impulses and forces. If Hitler could be characterized as "the leader of a frustrated people's vengeful dream" (*The War For Men's Minds*), and if Nazism itself was nothing less than the powerful eruption of fanatical mysticism and barbarism, then to counter this Grierson posits a strict totalitarian society based entirely on rationality, order, and discipline.

In Grierson's writings before and during the war, it is possible to detect an undercurrent of fear of human emotion, reflected in his propagandistic effort to provide an "emotional map" for the masses, "a pattern of thought and feeling" delivered from on high. Rigid control by authority must manage emotional content, which often goes by the name of "individualism" in his writings but which nonetheless constitutes the "Frankenstein" monster of "loosed energies and forces which it [individualism] is, of all philosophies least fitted to co-ordinate and control".[20]

In this context, it is interesting to examine a wartime film made specifically for children on the rural non-theatrical circuits. *Lesson in Living* (1944) uses a loosely fictional structure to depict the situation of a young boy named Bob who dislikes school, has a tendency to be truant, and prefers to spend his time alone, tinkering and fooling around. On a day when he does reluctantly attend school, he quietly carves his initials into his desk with a penknife. It is the same desk, it turns out, in which his father long ago carved his own initials. This scene of quiet rebellion and assertion of individuality (symbolized by Bob's initials) becomes the occasion for this particular "lesson in living". An external authority visiting the school observes Bob's quietly defiant act of rebellion and proceeds to patiently explain that "Bob should have spent his time *improving* the desk". Suitably chastened, Bob joins the other children in transforming a barn into a community centre for organized activities. The three activities mentioned in the film are playing basketball, holding Farm Forum meetings, and watching motion pictures.

The film's message is obvious. Individualism, a heritage from the past, leads to destructive acts. Rebellious emotion must be channelled into what the film calls "community energy" for "improvement". All activity, even leisure and play, must be organized, supervised, planned, and fully geared to social betterment. Anyone who deviates from this group "unity" is a destructive threat to the orderly march towards a better society for all. As Grierson believed, there can be no room for "the luxury of private deviation" or "the promiscuous exercise of mental or emotional interests". At the end of the film, the previously rebellious Bob dutifully sits in the darkened hall, watching a motion picture with the rest of the anonymous audience. Silenced and attentive, they listen to the voice-of-authority speaking from the screen.

A central tenet in the notion of sacrifice that Grierson proposed for the future is the strict repression of human emotion, coupled with the scientific management of that dimension of living by experts—including Hollywood, as well as the propagandists for the state. Organizing the moods of relaxation and resolution was a necessary part of his totalitarian vision. His writings speak constantly of a "bright future", "light", "hope", "the good", "faith", "improvement", "inspiration", "a more civilized world"—all terms which are vague enough to be read from any and every angle. But whatever their meaning, in the Griersonian vision these qualities depend on the absolute repression of their opposite pole. It is to this end that Grierson emphasizes work, rationality, order, discipline, the elimination of unruly emotion itself.

Not surprisingly, one searches in vain through the wartime NFB documentaries for references to the intense labour disputes and unrest occurring in Canada, especially at mid-war, or to the conscription crisis that was so central to the Mackenzie King political scene, or to the arrest and imprisonment of 22,000 Japanese-Canadians, or to the government policy of turning away virtually all Jewish refugees fleeing Europe. Those other taboo subjects, if explored on screen, would have challenged the central filmic construction of a "Canada" fully united without question in a total effort. In addition, however, these aspects of the domestic scene were fraught with emotional challenge to central authority. Each issue was clearly the site of private deviation motivated by intense personal feeling and personal experience. These taboo issues might be called the dark underside of the bright picture of technocratic order and discipline and unity represented in the films. These aspects of reality could not be mentioned because they embodied areas in which the master plan of democracy was being challenged by "the din of amateur judgment". Speculating on the necessary components of totalitarianism, Grierson wrote in 1943:

> Differences apart, both [Lenin and Hitler] make the argument that if and when total effort is vital to a society the unity of men's minds is as important as the unity of their energies and the democracies are today accepting this principle readily as a measure of war.[21]

Just as his simplistic analysis of the public's "moods of resolution and relaxation" allowed for no possibility of a "mood" of protest or criticism, so too the "unity of men's minds" would have to revolve around absolute consent.

At the top of Grierson's authoritarian structure of technocratic specialists is the media expert, whose role was not about to end with the war. Indeed, as Grierson wrote in "The Challenge of Peace" in 1945, the problems of dealing with "the subjective implications" of the technological revolution demanded media "specialists" who understood "the intangibles that affect the imaginations of men and determine their will". As he well knew, "It is a question of the images that direct men's vision and determine their loyalties, and we are concerned not only with the conscious processes of the mind but with the subconscious ones which insensibly govern the pattern of men's attention and the manner of their action."[22]

Thus, Grierson's totalitarianism was an odd mixture of a variety of political elements, foremost of which was the belief that the international integration of economies and technological enterprise, coordinated by state and corporate initiative and a technocracy of experts, might lead to a "new and interim society which is neither capitalist nor socialist", and thus seemingly beyond ideology.[23] This too is an ideology and one which was completely in line with the goals of multinational business. It is important to note that the Griersonian vision for the future gained no endorsement from one important circle of opinion. One of the main complaints about the wartime NFB's depiction of the Soviet Union on film—*Inside Fighting Russia* (1942), *Our Northern Neighbour* (1944), and in sequences included in other compilation films—came from the Soviet legation in Ottawa, which was not entirely flattered by its portrait.[24]

The world economy envisioned by Grierson would eliminate disorder on every level and introduce a "new dispensation of thought and habit". "The key to this new dispensation," he wrote, "may well be our use of the two words corporate and co-operative. They represent, it is possible, a new species of measurement and perspective and therefore a new species of power and thought and habit."[25]

If these two words, "corporate" and "co-operative", are the key to the "new dispensation", they are also a key to the Griersonian vision, though not without ambiguity. In the Griersonian lexicon, "co-operative" refers to the mass nature of modern society: the characteristic feature of the age by which work could be organized around mass production and increased efficiency, and mass allegiance to "patterns of thought and feeling" could be affected through mass media—radio and film, with TV on the horizon. The word "corporate", however, has a less clear meaning in his lexicon, though it recurs throughout his wartime speeches and writings.

One explanation of the word is provided by Bertram Gross, who indicates that the word "corporate" had a specific political nuance at the time:

> Although the classic fascists openly subverted constitutional democracy and flaunted their militarism, they took great pains to conceal the Big Capital–Big Government partnership. One device for doing this was the myth of "corporatism", or the "corporate State". In place of geographically elected parliaments, the Italians and the Germans set up elaborate systems whereby every interest in the country—including labor—was to be "functionally" represented. In fact, the main function was to provide facades behind which the decisions were made by intricate networks of business cartels working closely with military officers and their own people in civilian government.[26]

Though it is difficult to know to what extent Grierson's use of the word "corporate" entailed this meaning, it is nevertheless evident that his totalitarianism was based on a close partnership between the state and international business to advance the necessary technostructure. Through such integration of forces, Grierson believed that there might come about "the release of co-operative and corporate energies on a scale never dreamt of before":

> To consider this simply as a temporary device of war is to mistake its significance and by doing so to dishearten the people; for it is what people in their hearts have been harking for and represents the fulfilment of an era. Total war may yet appear as the dreadful period of forced apprenticeship in which we learned what we had hitherto refused to learn, how to order the vast new forces of human and material energies to decent human ends.[27]

Presumably, for Grierson this "fulfilment of an era" would launch capitalism into its most modernist, "progressive" stage—beyond individualism, nationalism, and (with scientific and technocratic planning) even beyond ideology. In this sense, Grierson's totalitarianism played directly into the hands of the U.S. multinationals, which had a similar, if more cynical, view of themselves as being beyond ideology.

In his 1983 book, *Trading With The Enemy,* Charles Higham documents the wartime existence of what he calls "The Fraternity", a group of Allied businessmen, financiers, and government officials whose "internationalist" allegiances prompted them to trade with both sides at war, making deals with the Nazis and fascist-owned or -controlled businesses throughout World War II.[28] In this Fraternity, whose members all "were represented internationally by the National City Bank or by the Chase National Bank", Higham identifies several key U.S. multinational corporations, including Standard Oil of New Jersey and the Chase National Bank (both Rockefeller concerns), the Ford Motor Company, ITT, General Motors, Du Pont, General Electric, Sterling Products (better known for its pharmaceuticals Bayer Aspirin and Phillips Milk of Magnesia), RCA (parent company for NBC), and a number of officials within the U.S. and British governments.[29] The existence of The Fraternity was entirely covered up by the U.S. government both during and after the war. As Higham writes:

> What would have happened if millions of American and British people, struggling with coupons and lines at the gas stations, had learned that in 1942 Standard Oil of New Jersey managers shipped the enemy's fuel

> through neutral Switzerland and that the enemy was shipping Allied fuel? Suppose the public had discovered that the Chase Bank in Nazi-occupied Paris after Pearl Harbor was doing millions of dollars' worth of business with the enemy with the full knowledge of the head office in Manhattan? Or that Ford trucks were being built for the German occupation troops in France with authorization from Dearborn, Michigan? Or that Colonel Sosthenes Behn, the head of the international American telephone conglomerate ITT, flew from New York to Madrid to Berne during the war to help improve Hitler's communications systems and improve the robot bombs that devastated London? Or that ITT built the Focke-Wulfs that dropped bombs on British and American troops? Or that crucial ball bearings were shipped to Nazi-associated customers in Latin America with the collusion of the vice-chairman of the U.S. War Production Board in partnership with Goring's cousin in Philadelphia when American forces were desperately short of them? Or that such arrangements were known about in Washington and either sanctioned or deliberately ignored?[30]

At least one of these arrangements had come under investigation by a U.S. senate committee in 1941: the business agreement between Standard Oil and Germany's I.G. Farben, the petrochemical giant.[31] I.G. Farben was known to have built its own concentration camp adjacent to Auschwitz—I.G. Auschwitz, as it was called by its directors—where camp labour was literally worked to death in the production of artificial rubber for the Reich's military needs.[32] Though some members of the U.S. senate investigating committee were appalled by the Standard–I.G. Farben agreement, so "lacking in patriotic concern", nothing seems to have come of the investigation. As Collier and Horowitz write, Rockefeller "had become a citizen above suspicion".[33]

A better explanation is provided by Higham. Writing about Standard Oil's transactions with Nazi Germany, he quotes from a December 26, 1941 message from the U.S. ambassador to Britain, John G. Winant:

> 'Embassy concurs with British view that on balance there is no reason for taking action which would at most be only minor irritant to Germans and which might complicate an already difficult situation or lead to unfortunate consequences as regards to future operations of American and British oil companies.'[34]

Behind such self-serving politics, there was also, according to Bertram Gross, the prevailing view that "top business circles sincerely believed 'Better Hitler than Stalin'".[35] Despite the presence of a Soviet ally during the war, multinational business's fear of communism outflanked even aversion to the spectre of the Third Reich and the horror of Nazi atrocities, which after all were no real threat to business as business. U.S. investments in Nazi Germany at the time of Pearl Harbor amounted to some $475 million, with Standard Oil ($210 million), General Motors ($35 million), ITT ($30 million), and Ford ($17.5 million) each concerned to ensure their German holdings against the spectre of the Communist menace.[36]

Such behind-the-scenes alignments obviously raise far-ranging questions about Canadian complicity in the deals. Though Higham's text makes no reference to Canada, the Department of Munitions and Supply was working closely with the U.S. War Production Board during the last three years of the war.[37] In addition, Howe's department was closely aligned with Canadian branch-plants of The Fraternity companies. Higham's revelations also raise questions about Grierson's knowledge of these activities.

Whether he knew or not, Grierson's political position seems not to have been at variance with the plans of at least some members of The Fraternity. In the immediate postwar period, after Grierson had left the NFB, funding for his New York-based film unit, The World Today Inc., was provided by a grant from the Rockefeller Foundation—indicating at least that his wartime politics and policies had not alienated him from the top U.S. business circles at the time.[38]

In his essay "The Documentary Idea" Grierson wrote, "The act is everything":

> *Die tat ist alles.* To put it in its simplest and naivest form—which is still good to remember and maintain—correct political change will be that alignment of political principles and loyalties which, given the circumstances of the world today, will best serve the interest of peoples of all lands, and the British people in proportion, and actively mobilize the native heart and mind to these ends. It will be that alignment which actively eliminates the evil forces, wherever they may be, which are against such interests, and all decadent forces, wherever they may be, which are not competent to control the developing scene. That is something on which all healthy elements must agree, and the unhealthy elements present events are sufficiently taking care of.[39]

The ambiguity of his closing sentence, which is almost chilling in its abstraction, calls for an examination of the possible "unhealthy elements" in wartime Canada. Of equal importance is the extent to which Grierson's "unhealthy elements" coincided with the diagnosis made by his employer. Mackenzie King had long been preoccupied with "those individuals who are life-destroying germs in human society"; in his third term, he set out to assist "the white corpuscles" of the body politic.[40]

8

The Anxious Mosaic

'Total war' is said to require 'total effort' but this has not been easily come by in nations which still have a hang-over of nineteenth-century thinking and laisser-faire. At a hundred points today wrong attitudes are still being taught: some in innocence of the dynamic change which total effort involves, some in conscious defence of the sectional and selfish interests which total effort must necessarily eliminate.

JOHN GRIERSON, 1942

On June 27, 1937, two days before his visit with Hitler, Prime Minister Mackenzie King made a revealing entry in his diary. He had been talking with Sir Neville Henderson, British ambassador in Berlin, and was enough impressed by one of Henderson's statements that he later recorded it for himself: "There is a lot England can learn from Germany in the treatment of the masses of the people."[1] In an era of competing totalitarian visions, control of the masses seems to have been on everyone's mind. The official onset of war allowed for this desire for control to express itself in a variety of ways.

By 1940, Great Britain was using its powers of state to rid itself of its own undesirables, including the arrest of some 30,000 refugees from Nazi Germany and Austria, most of them Jews, socialists, and trade unionists.[2] In that same year, Britain began using Canada as a convenient penal colony, sending a first load of 3,000 POWs and 4,000 civilian "enemy aliens" for internment. Eric Koch has documented that there were 2,290 Jewish escapees from Hitler included among those first 7,000 people interned by Canada for Great Britain, a fact that sheds more light on the Mackenzie King Cabinet's policy of silence on "the Jewish question", on the Canadian immigration department's refusal to accept Jewish refugees up to and during the war, and the NFB's wartime silence on Nazi racial policy and persecution.[3]

Perhaps inspired by the boldness of Britain's internment measures, Mackenzie King moved to silence and curtail some undesirables of his own. By an order-in-council on January 11, 1940, the minister of justice had been given the authority to arrest and detain without trial anyone "acting in any manner prejudicial to the public safety or the safety of the State".[4] Under these sweeping regulations, the government proceeded to arrest more than 100 trade union and labour activists, who were jailed in 1940 and 1941 without charges and without hearings for up to two years.[5] Though the order-in-council ultimately led to the arrest of 2,241 Canadians in the first years of the war, the primary focus seems to have been on labour organizing and the Red Menace, which was presumably threatening corporate desires. As Eric Koch writes in *Deemed Suspect,* the Canadian authorities were "far more worried about the communists than about Nazis in the [internment] camps".[6] Moreover, as early as 1937, Canadian Minister of Defence Ian Mackenzie had been drawing up plans for the arrest of various citizens deemed suspect by the state.[7]

Throughout the war, Britain proceeded to send some 25,000 more POWs to internment camps in Canada.[8] Meanwhile, Mackenzie King continued his policy of arresting troublesome Canadians, including Mennonites on the Prairies, whose religion forbade participation in wars,[9] and more than 22,000 Japanese-Canadians on the west coast. In *The Politics of Racism,* Ann Gomer Sunahara focusses on the economic factors behind Mackenzie King's action. According to her research, the massive arrests and the state seizure of the property of Japanese-Canadians were fully to the benefit of, and motivated by, Anglo-Canadian economic interests.[10] In some cases, the internments also coincided with the government's anti-union measures.

For example, much of the focus for the arrest of labour activists was on the Prairies, where attempts to organize Hungarian, Slovak, Czecho-Slovak, and Ukrainian field workers were a threat to Anglo-Canadian capital in the region. The internment of the labour leaders among these workers, as well as the confiscation and closure of Ukrainian labour halls by the Custodian of Enemy Property, broke up this threat to the dominant powers. In the case of the Alberta Sugar Beet Workers' Union, the growers' opposition to the union was well served by the massive relocation of arrested Japanese-Canadians to the area. As a captive population put to work, they became "an ideal solution to [the growers'] labour problems".[11]

According to Barry Broadfoot, at the time many Canadians were completely unaware of these arrests.[12] Nevertheless, with some 50,000 internees in camps across the country, it must have been obvious, at least to their neighbouring communities, that the Mackenzie King state was concerned about "unity" in trying times. Ironically, this was a part of the context for a key Griersonian initiative: the establishment of wartime non-theatrical circuits—whose operation is often used by Canadian film scholars to temper Grierson's "totalitarianism".[13] In a 1940 CBC broadcast, Grierson referred to the National Film Act and his goal: "The National Film Board will be *the eyes of Canada*. It will, through a national use of cinema, see Canada and see it whole—its people and its purposes."[14] Those "eyes", however, were entirely unseeing when it came to the internment camps, another in the growing list of taboo subjects for wartime films.

In 1941, with the "Canada Carries On" series being screened on a regular basis in urban movie theatres across Canada, Grierson instituted plans for the "supplementary" distribution and exhibition arrangements which had been on his mind since his 1927 tour of France and Germany for the Empire Marketing Board. In consultation with Herbert Lash, who was at the time the director of public information (a position Grierson himself would fill in 1943 as director of wartime information), Grierson outlined his plan to hire projectionists to travel throughout the country and screen 16mm films for audiences who might not otherwise be reached by the war propaganda.[15]

During the war, some 150 to 170 travelling projectionists (including five women) were hired by the NFB to show films on these non-theatrical circuits. Each projectionist was responsible for bringing a monthly 16mm basic film program (selected by Ottawa) to the designated locations on his or her circuit. The NFB rural circuits, instituted in 1942, included country schools, rural churches and town halls, mining and lumber camps, and northern outposts. The NFB industrial circuits (instituted in 1943) reached workers in urban factories and shipyards. The NFB trade union circuits (1943) brought films to trade union halls for screening after union meetings. With the exception of the five women hired, the projectionists were primarily men who had passed the age of military service and who, in many cases, had experience in education or film society work.

The non-theatrical circuits were intended to serve those "national purposes" discussed in the House of Commons during the debate on the 1939 National Film Act. As Minister of Trade and Commerce W.D. Euler stated, there was a need for "the distribution of national films designed to help Canadians in all parts of Canada to understand the ways of living and problems of Canadian people". More succinctly, as Euler and a host of other politicians and business leaders had told Grierson during his 1938 tour of Canada, there was a need to "diminish sectionalism".

That desire becomes clearer in official wartime correspondence about the rural circuits, the first of the non-theatrical circuits organized in 1942. The co-ordinator in charge of the rural circuits during the war was Donald Buchanan, who had been active in the Film Society movement since 1935 and who later helped Grierson obtain captured enemy film footage for recutting by the NFB.[16] In a promotional article for the new rural circuits, Buchanan explained that "the talking picture, with its combined appeal of voice and visual image, was [according to Grierson and Lash] the best medium for carrying the message of fighting Canada to all those communities of varied racial origin which make up rural Canada, from east to west."[17] Another wartime piece by Buchanan is more explicit:

> About 300 of the points served by rural circuits consist of farming areas populated by Canadians of foreign origin. Here the real test of the documentary movie comes. Will these people respond to its stimulus.[18]

Anglo-Canadian anxiety about "these people" is also evident in official correspondence on the selection of circuit itineraries. For example, a letter of November 7, 1942, sent to local authorities by one of the NFB regional directors, reads: "We have made a special attempt ... to put these programmes in districts where we considered the need was greatest, i.e., outlying rural districts and in districts where foreign-born predominate."[19] Buchanan also wrote: "The object of these rural circuits was two-fold. First, to bring people in remote settlements into visual contact with the War, and secondly, to stimulate greater knowledge of and interest in current events among foreign language groups."[20]

The specific targetting of "foreign born", "communities of varied racial origin", and "foreign language groups" (that is, other than English-speaking) indicates that the project may be seen within the larger context of Anglo-Canadian dominance and the continuing fear of the Red Menace. It was precisely in the proposed audiences for the wartime non-theatrical circuits—the regions, with their "foreign born", and the Canadian labour movement—that threats to "unity" were perceived to exist. These are the references for what Grierson subtly termed "sectional and selfish interests" in need of elimination. Presumably, "foreign born" and "foreign language groups" did not have the same tradition of colonial allegiance to Great Britain that was motivating the Anglo-Canadian population. Nor was Canadian labour fully and unquestionably aligned to the needs of the Canadian state. Grierson, with his understanding of the role of film in the assimilation process, his propagandist's abilities in "the manufacture of consent", and his vision of the new form of democracy necessary in a modern age, was the right man to attempt to deal with "sectional and selfish interests" across Canada.

The rural circuits were launched in January 1942, with the first 30 circuits served by travelling projectionists set up in the prairie provinces. The evening program of film was usually 90 minutes in length, with the basic slate of films selected by a central committee in Ottawa. The first program consisted of five films: *Peoples of Canada, Heroes of the Atlantic, Ottawa on the River, Toilers of the Grand Banks,* and the Disney film, *The Thrifty Pig.*[21] As a first organized screening, this program set the tone for the project. *Peoples of Canada* (March 1941) was a production from Associated Screen News, directed by Gordon Sparling with Stuart Legg as associate producer. The film was a three-reel effort, the first in a series, portraying components of the Canadian population and their typical lifestyle and employment: the Scots, Dutch, Germans, Scandinavians, Doukhobors, Hutterites, Mennonites, Chinese, native Indian, Inuit, and the Québecois. As Evans notes, the series (1941-43) struck a note of "tolerance for others", though its portrait of the Québecois ignored the thousands of urbanites to concentrate on "the Quebecker as a farmer whose church was at the centre of community life".[22] *Heroes of the Atlantic* (May 1941) was an installment in the "Canada Carries On" series, a compilation film which explored the work of the British Merchant Navy, and one of its guardians, the Royal Canadian Navy, in the battle of the Atlantic. *Ottawa on the River* (1941) was a season-by-season portrait of the capital with a very leisurely tone and a tourist focus on the sights of a picturesque city. Obviously compiled from footage shot previously by the Government Motion Picture Bureau, the film conveys a quiet and orderly capital city very different from the portrait in a later work, *Ottawa, Wartime Capital* (1942). *Toilers of the Grand Banks* (1940) explored the work of fishermen on the east coast catching cod in the Atlantic. *The Thrifty Pig* (1941) was a Disney animation film encouraging Canadians to save their money for the War Bond drive in support of the war effort. The film was one of the coproductions with Disney quietly funded by the NFB.

As a first program, this slate of films reveals the expected focus of the project: the diversity of the Canadian population and the need for tolerance, Canadian support for the British war effort, the centrality of Ottawa, the necessity for financing the war effort through War Bonds. There is nothing surprising in such a selection for the "federal use of film", though the only two colour films on the program, *Ottawa on the River* and *The Thrifty Pig,* undoubtedly had a stronger impact on the audiences.

In a larger context, the program reveals some significant undercurrents. With the government itself showing a remarkable intolerance for diversity of views, especially on the Prairies, the effect of preaching "tolerance for others" through a mechanism of the state may have seemed somewhat hypocritical to audiences. There was also the exclusion, in the "Peoples of Canada" series, of two ethnic communities perhaps most in need of tolerance at the time: Jewish-Canadians and Japanese-Canadians. But a film reference to either group would have been too close to real issues during the war; the filmic construction of a unified "Canada" was not intended to hinge on the exploration of actual circumstances. Another absence in the "Peoples of Canada" depiction is the Anglo-colonial populace. As the dominant group, it is the norm by which ethnicity and "otherness" were defined. Perhaps for this reason Grierson and his NFB colleagues saw no need to examine the lens through which the other peoples of Canada were seen.

Once the non-theatrical rural circuits had been launched in the Prairie provinces, there was a concerted effort to expand them across the country as quickly as possible. That expansion depended on "tight supervision from the top", with NFB head office in Ottawa controlling the rural circuits for a co-ordinated and centralized effort in total war.[23] In line with Grierson's views on the co-operative or mass nature of modernist society, there was a need for the construction of a mass audience aligned with central authority. That desired construction is apparent in several aspects of the wartime rural circuits.

First, every travelling projectionist showed the same monthly film selections to the 20 localities on his or her circuit. As one wartime projectionist later recalled, "It was very interesting but it was a grind job. There wasn't much selectivity to it. It was running the films we had, and we had these basic programmes in those days."[24] As Donald Buchanan, who was in charge of the wartime rural circuits, wrote at the time:

> How are the programmes composed? There has to be a new group of films each month. They have to be made up to appeal to every race and section of the nation; for example, Trois Pistoles, Quebec, views the same subjects as does Salmon Arm, British Columbia.[25]

Thus, at the peak of the war, with at least 92 rural circuits in operation, some 1,840 communities across Canada were being served by the travelling projectionists, each one showing the same basic slate of films.[26]

This role of centralized authority in Ottawa was also mirrored at the local level.

> Initial instructions to the projectionists were to contact the school principal, the mayor, the chairman of the local War Savings Committee, or some other dignitary who was looked upon as the leader in that community, to secure his endorsement and support for the film programs.... It was expected that someone would speak on the Victory Loan campaign, or on some other aspect of local community activity to support the war effort, during each film showing.[27]

But even these "local" talks were fully centralized, with lecture notes provided from Ottawa. As official correspondence at the time explained:

> In order that the greatest value may be obtained from these programmes from a citizenship point of view, arrangements are being made to have the school principal, the minister or some other public-spirited and qualified citizen give a short talk of not more than fifteen minutes in connection with each programme. Lecture notes which will serve as the basis for such talks are being supplied for the use of these individuals. These notes have been prepared by the Canadian Council Of Education For Citizenship.[28]

Obviously, the Anglo-colonial bourgeoisie was going all out in its efforts for "unity". But Grierson, with his authoritarian vision of control of the masses by experts, was also constructing a communication framework by which, at least during wartime, such control might be attempted.

This view of the wartime rural circuits is by no means the prevailing one in Canadian film scholarship. Both Gary Evans and Ian Lockerbie, for example, temper Grierson's totalitarianism by referring to his presumed belief in two-way communication. Lockerbie writes:

> Even when [Grierson] puts forward one of his rashest ideas that you can be 'totalitarian for good' as well as for evil—a risky notion if there ever was one—it is qualified by saying that there has to be a two-way traffic between the people and the State. The fundamental safeguard against the abuse of propaganda is that the State should draw as much information and guidance from the people as the other way around.[29]

Similarly, Evans states:

> In developing his idea of communication, he [Grierson] was careful to avoid having the few preach to the many. Information was a two-way process between state and people, people and state. He would encourage the two-way process of communication in the years of the Second World War, in the non-theatrical film circuits of Canada and in the regular use of polls to report the tenor of public opinion to the government. His belief was that the group of filmmakers which came to be called documentary were specialists for and on behalf of people and not specialists from without.[30]

Grierson's views on the "ten million amateur thinkers" in Canada during the war and the ways in which "the din of their amateur judgment" was slowing down progress make it somewhat hard to believe that he would be terribly interested in "guidance from the people". Rather, it seems more the case that Grierson was careful to try to avoid the appearance of having the few preach to the many. Like any modern propaganda maestro, he knew that "democracy" must provide the illusion of two-way communication, that "the manufacture of consent" depends on a mass citizenry believing that it has some actual voice and impact on decisions, events, and planning. The importance of public opinion in modern times—what Mackenzie King recognized as the difference between force and consent—hinges on the appearance of two-way communication. In this sense, certain features of the wartime rural circuits were important for creating the semblance of a local voice in a centralized structure.

So, for example, the dissemination of lecture notes from Ottawa meant that the words and viewpoint from on high were to be voiced by local citizens addressing local audiences. At each circuit point, a local film committee chairman was appointed, whose responsibility it was to provide a summary of audience reaction to the projectionist, who then submitted a monthly report to Ottawa, entitled "Last Month On My

Circuit".[31] Such local feedback tended at times, however, to closely follow the official line. One local chairman summarized audience response to the November 1942 slate of films, which included *Fighting Fields, Battle Is Our Business,* and *Forward Commando*:

> Give them this class of war pictures and do not spare the public from the sordid details of war. It is the only way the public in the West will know there is a war on. The war has not touched thousands of them and many are inclined to look at it in a very detached way. Scores of them will not buy Victory Bonds when they could well afford it. Every excuse possible is offered why they cannot buy. They either served themselves in the last war, have sons in this war, or expect to fight in some 'future war'. Such are the excuses for not buying. In addition to this, many are pulling every possible string to keep their sons out of the fighting forces.[32]

Any number of other citizens in this community would have summarized audience response to the screenings quite differently, without such a commitment to total effort.

Another technique for creating local feedback was the incorporation of discussion-trailers at the end of certain films.[33] There were 17 of these trailers made during the war. The only one of these discussion trailers that I've seen, the trailer following *Battle Is Their Birthright,* is highly prescriptive in tone, dissuading viewers from the "ultra-nationalism" of "dedicating themselves to Canada". One travelling projectionist, E.A. Fraser, who served provinces on the east coast, later recalled that the audience reception to such instruction was "mixed to say the least" and that sometimes the discussion-trailers were followed by a "stoney silence". Fraser remembered receiving a sharp rebuke from a local member of the provincial government, who said, "We like to come to your movies but we also like to keep our thoughts to ourselves." According to Fraser, other travelling projectionists met with similar responses to the discussion-trailers.[34] An audience can usually detect when its participation is being sought, not to actually affect decisions made on high, but to create a sense of local involvement.

A third procedure often pointed to as proof of the two-way process at work in the circuits is more difficult to assess. The prevailing view is that ideas for films came in to the NFB from the audiences themselves. Wartime filmmaker Evelyn Spice Cherry recalls this "flow-back from the people":

> At the time it was simply tremendous. Through our distribution system we had the most splendid flow of enthusiasm and ideas for films coming

> back from the people. (A great deal of the work of Helen Watson). We didn't sit in committees or consultations and decide what the films would be. The film ideas came in, and then we sat and talked about how we could do it.[35]

However, wartime filmmaker Margaret Ann Adamson (Elton) has clarified the nature of the decision-making process:

> If it was filtered back that there was a need for a film on a certain subject it usually tied in with a request, perhaps from a government department, or perhaps an intuition of Grierson's. Grierson felt very strongly that his role as Commissioner demanded that he keep the so-called creative people well and truly in check to keep them from doing their own thing, and that the chief aspect of his public duty was to serve the government departments. So he knew pretty well what they needed. Then, if this was reinforced from the regions and from different areas and provinces, the film that needed to be made got made.[36]

The other argument that Lockerbie uses to "refute the charge" that Grierson was totalitarian in both theory and practice is "the strength of Grierson's attachment to the local and the particular, which is a central thread in his allegiance to a realist aesthetic".[37] It is difficult to find in the films themselves much interest in the local and the particular. The prestige series (re-released for the circuits), for example, were far more concerned with conveying a "world viewpoint" and "editorial internationalism". Although some of the 16mm films for the circuits incorporated the local and the particular in the shooting process, the ideological emphasis in the films consistently points the viewer away from local ways and local differences. Grierson's supposed "attachment to the local and the particular" was primarily expressed, not in some realist aesthetic, but in getting the films to the localities, which was the function of the circuits.

Not surprisingly, there was a degree of resistance and even resentment on the part of audiences targetted for the rural circuits. C.W. Gray included this passage in an early draft of his text about the circuits: "The writer recalls early visits in certain rural areas in 1942 where many people in the first audiences were, to say the least, apathetic if not down-right negative."[38] Quebec travelling projectionist Jacques Ste-Marie later remembered audience response in this way: "'They're all propaganda films, government propaganda films', I could hear them say, 'so few French production films'."[39] Vaughn Deacon, Ontario NFB wartime regional representative, later admitted: "The actual rural circuit thing was almost completely an artificial concept. I had the greatest difficulty here in persuading people. On the face of it, it makes no sense. The men often found it difficult to get an adult audience."[40]

Recent research by Peter Morris reveals that this lack of audience attendance was to some extent covered up by Grierson's wartime NFB. "There is good evidence to suggest that NFB audience claims during Grierson's tenure were highly exaggerated at best and knowingly false at worst."[41] Official claims of an audience of 6 million for the non-theatrical circuits in the last year of the war must be tempered by scepticism, as well as by later NFB admissions that virtually half the wartime rural audience was the country-school population.[42] Nevertheless, even an audience of 3 million (half the official claim) would be sizable in a country of 11 million people, and the country-school population during the war was by no means an insignificant audience.

The reasons why the wartime rural circuits were relatively unsuccessful with their intended audience may be found in the films themselves, with their Griersonian emphasis on the need to obey central authority and expert planners. This is apparent in many of the films devoted to farming practices. *Bacon for Britain* (1943), *Do Unto Animals* (1939), *Farm Front* (1943), *Farm Improvement Series* (1944), *Farmers' Forum* (1942), *Hands for the Harvest* (1943), *New Plans for the Land* (1943) all stress new scientific methods to achieve greater and more efficient yields. But underneath this message is another: individual and regional variations in practice are unacceptable, outdated, and an impediment to central authority's co-ordination.

A similar problem appears in circuit films geared to the rural housewife. These films, which focus on meal preparation under wartime rationing and on how to remake old clothes, seem patronizing and redundant for audiences who had lived through ten debilitating years of economic depression. Nevertheless, the wartime NFB was building a genre in films like *Four New Apple Dishes* (1942), *Vitamin Films* (1943), *What Makes Us Grow* (1943), *The Main Dish* (1943), *Get Your Vitamins* (1943), *When Do We Eat* (1944), *Supper's Ready* (1944), *Thought for Food* (1943), *Make It Over* (1943), *Stitch and Save* (1943). Many of these films were in the "Knife and Fork" series sponsored by the Wartime Information Board and the Wartime Prices and Trade Board. According to Evans, the series "was a response to what Grierson referred to as the necessity of harmonizing producers' and consumers' viewpoint".[43] But even in these mundane topics, it is possible to detect the real message: conformity to the dictates of modern science as dispensed by central authority. In this case, it is the science of home economics, or domestic science as it was called at the time. Amateur or foreign ways of doing household chores were to be replaced by methods developed in laboratories and standardized for all. The white-coated domestic scientist, a recurring figure in the films, demonstrates the more efficient techniques (and the new home appliances) of modern household management.

Such films were slightly out of touch with the actual lives of many Canadians. As one farmer described his wartime effort:

> Two sections and me running the whole show and all these government boards always on your back. Grow more wheat, grow more barley to keep more pigs, and more milk for powdered milk and cheese and the whole list, and on one hand they're working you to death and on the other, they're raising taxes, and I think it was 10 percent they wanted out of you for war bonds. And try as you did, it was like pulling teeth trying to get tractor parts, let alone a new tractor.[44]

In such a context, it is hard to imagine any massive turnout for an evening once a month to hear Ottawa's instructions on more modern methods for living.

In many of the films made for the rural circuits, there is a correct way of doing virtually everything, whether it is mailing a letter (*Canadian Mail,* 1943), using food coupons (*Coupon Value,* 1943), planting a garden (*The Plots Thicken,* 1944), or blowing one's nose (*The Nose Has It,* 1942). Central authority seems to have overlooked little in the name of effective discipline and planning. Apparently, "wrong attitudes" could be found in any number of individual or regional deviations.

If the tone of many of the wartime circuit films could be called authoritarian, another group of films for the rural circuits is somewhat paternalistic. Films like *Farmers of the Prairies* (1940), *Gaspé Cod Fishermen* (1944), *Grand Manan* (1943), *Iceland on the Prairies* (1941), *Land of Quebec* (1944), *New Scotland* (1944), *Peace River* (1941), *People of Blue Rocks* (1941), *Poland on the Prairies* (1944), *Toilers of the Grand Banks* (1940) do convey the great variety of traditions, peoples, and ways of life contributing to the Canadian mosaic. And yet, for all the beauty of many of the films, there is also something odd about them. Helen Watson Gordon, an administrator for the rural circuits, later recalled:

> The films we were showing on the rural circuits did a great deal to bring about national unity. We were working among the ten or fifteen different ethnic groups that were settled in specific areas around the country.

> Ukrainians, Mennonites, all of them. And we were showing one group to the other, say the fishermen in Nova Scotia to the farmers in the prairies. We were telling Canada about Canadians and at the same time we were introducing different groups to a country that was going to be their home.[45]

In part, the films have an oddness about them because there is virtually no reference to contemporary problems affecting these regional groups. Perhaps because Gordon singles out Ukrainians and Mennonites in her statement, it's hard not to think of the actual circumstances in their lives at the time, and especially with regard to actions by the state. Films about folk-dancing and crafts and traditional occupations of such "ethnic groups" seem beside the point, even vaguely unreal. Contemporary audiences may also have sensed this unreality and the propagandist intent beneath it.

These regional portraits seem odd and somewhat unreal also because some used Grierson's compilation technique, incorporating footage shot years before the war by the Government Motion Picture Bureau. Thus, it is never clear whether scenes are 1940s footage of these regions or vintage material included to create (in the stereotypical sense) a predominant image of a region.

There is, as well, something nostalgic in these portraits, particularly in contrast to other films shown on the circuits with their emphasis on science, technology, and modern production. It is as though these ethnographic films depict, by comparison, the old ways of life that were once significant to the country in its regional stage, but that in wartime and thereafter would be outmoded and simply quaint. This nostalgia is further enhanced by the films' avoidance of any references to the real political turmoil, dissension, problems, and difficulties at the time. It might be fair to say that such films evoked Canada's regionalism in order to subtly subvert it by exposing its old-fashioned quaintness in the modernist context. Such old-fashioned regional portraits—for example, the predominant portrait of Quebec as a rural, traditional, church-centred collectivity of simple folk—also underlined the "need" for paternal guidance by expert authority.

Grierson's choice of the compilation film model, with its voice-of-authority narration, was perhaps another factor that alienated audiences on the rural circuits. Films from the re-released prestige series, with their world viewpoint, their emphasis on technology, and their insistent voice-overs, may have seemed too remote and prescriptive. As one local film committee chairman expressed poignantly to C.W. Gray, "Occasional shots of known individuals working in factories, mines, or otherwise would give public appeal—letting him speak."[46] Although some of the films about the Canadian armed services did make an attempt to identify specific individuals on screen, and even at times let them speak via syncsound, this aspect of labour identity is generally lacking in the wartime films. There is, rather, an unavoidable sense of an anonymous mass quietly toiling to serve the corporate state.

The need to diminish sectionalism and promote unity thus resulted in a wartime rural circuit structure in which communication was directed from centre to regions, from experts to amateurs, from Anglo-Canadian authority to foreign-born and foreign-language groups. If, in Vaughn Deacon's words, this was "almost completely an artificial concept", it was nevertheless one which fit Grierson's belief that "the din of amateur judgment" should not paralyze "progressive democracy".

The other aspect of Canadian society that was hindering the "dynamic change which total effort involves" was the Canadian labour movement, with its "selfish" interests and "wrong attitudes" standing in the way of Griersonian progress. Once the rural circuits had gotten underway in 1942, plans for industrial and trade union circuits were next on the agenda.

The first NFB industrial circuits were located in Quebec, a province containing one-third of the wartime population, but also the scene of both anti-conscription sentiment and massive labour disputes in the munitions and aircraft industries. The industrial circuits were organized in Quebec early in 1943 (the logical place to begin to eliminate sectional and selfish interests), then in Ontario, and finally in the other provinces. Like the rural circuits, the industrial circuits were served by travelling projectionists, who screened films in factories and shipyards during lunch breaks and shift changes. With industry operating 24 hours a day, there were several occasions each day for screenings. Within a few months, trade union circuits were instituted, and films were shown in trade union halls after meetings. It is probably no coincidence that the institution of both these circuits coincided with the worst year of labour unrest Canada had seen since 1919.

Mackenzie King's creation of the company union for the Rockefellers during World War I had proved an effective tool for preventing the growth of independent unions in the postwar years. Through his labour-management conciliation boards, companies could appear to be sharing their managerial power with labour, while at the same time retaining virtual control over unorganized employees. Behind the hostility towards unions there was more than the fear of higher wages. As Desmond Morton writes:

> A union prevented an employer from hiring, firing, setting wages, demanding overtime, or, for that matter, granting a half-holiday as his own whim or convenience dictated. Behind the strikes and violence, the yellow-dog contracts, the company unions, the goons and vigilantes there was usually one brutal struggle: whether or not a union could force recognition from an employer.[47]

With his experience in industrial relations and immigration, Mackenzie King had accurately predicted the post–World War I milieu and the ways in which the availability of new labour could be exploited to defeat union drives. In the United States, it was not until 1933 that unionism received any real support from governmental initiative.

The U.S. National Industrial Recovery Act promised that "employees shall have the right to organize and bargain collectively through representatives of their own choosing and shall be free from interference, restraint and coercion."[48] For the first time in U.S. history, legislation was in place that asserted the necessity for real collective bargaining. When the section proved unenforceable, Senator Robert Wagner helped push the National Labour Relations Act through Congress, turning rhetoric into law. Unions that could win majority support from workers were certifiable as legal bargaining agents and protected from management interference in their activities.

> The Wagner Act made possible the explosion of union organizing in the United States after 1935. For Canadian workers, it provided the model legislation they desperately needed in order to share in the gains of unionism. However, through the re-election of Mackenzie King in 1935, Canadians could expect nothing more than fusty reiterations of the merits of the Industrial Disputes Investigation Act.[49]

Though U.S. companies were thereby forced by law to accept a legal process through which workers could choose their own bargaining agent, this did not necessarily mean there was peace and accord in subsequent industrial relations.

Irénée du Pont—brother of Lammot du Pont, GM director—used

General Motors money to finance the notorious Black Legion, a terrorist organization designed to prevent autoworkers from unionizing.[50] The members wore hoods and black robes with skull and crossbones; they bombed union meetings, murdered union organizers, and "dedicated their lives to destroying Jews and Communists".[51] As well, du Pont personally paid almost $1 million from his own pocket "for armed and gas-equipped storm troops modeled on the Gestapo to sweep through [GM] plants and beat up anyone who proved rebellious".[52]

Although the Wagner Act opened a window of opportunity for unionism in the United States, a window which at least some American companies were trying to close, their branch-plant companies in Canada were intent on preventing any union gains. Especially active in the struggle to defeat Canadian unionism before and during the war were the branch plants of the U.S. companies in The Fraternity, Charles Higham's term for those multinationals that maintained active business arrangements with Nazi Germany right through World War II. Their efforts to defeat Canadian unionism found a willing partner in the Canadian state. As Desmond Morton writes, "For all the prime minister's protestations of affection for the workers, his government soon appeared to be vigorously anti-union."[53]

The Oshawa strike at General Motors in 1937 was a prewar indication of the need for more corporate control. Although the strike has been hailed as "the birth of industrial unionism in Canada", it also initiated a period of more intense lobbying by corporate industry at the federal level.[54] The establishing of Local 222 of the United Auto Workers at Oshawa's General Motors plant was the occasion for corporate forces to rally to prevent anything similar to the Wagner Act from being instituted in Canada. Because the legislation in the United States barred corporate management from a long list of unfair and oppressive anti-union practices, from firing union sympathizers to promoting a company union, it was a model that went firmly against the Rockefeller Plan as designed by Mackenzie King.

In 1939, Mackenzie King, who needed to appear to be the friend of labour without alienating corporate industry, finally gave approval to a longstanding private bill from J.S. Woodsworth.[55] For the first time in Canadian history, it became a criminal offence to fire an employee who supported union activities. But as George Burt of the United Auto Workers later observed, "They fired you and said it was because you weren't doing a good job in the plant! Employers could do what they liked. We had no assurance of anything."[56]

After the declaration of war, co-operation between government and business became even more entrenched. One government measure early in the war was the extension of the Industrial Disputes Investigation Act, with its delaying effect on strikes, to all national wartime industries.[57]

> Another step, Privy Council Order 2685, declared that fair and reasonable standards of wages and working conditions *should* be observed and the right of the workers to form their own unions *should* be recognized. Greeted with pleasure by Canadian union leaders, it soon proved to be an empty gesture.[58]

Without legislation like the Wagner Act to back up such recommendations, employers simply ignored the order. As Ray Stevenson of the United Steelworkers later recalled, "During that entire period there was nothing that said that even if you organized a mine 100 percent that the company had to sit down and bargain. The only way you could compel the recognition of the union was the strike weapon."[59] When the Canadian Congress of Labour complained that employers were simply ignoring the Privy Council order, Mackenzie King's minister of labour, Norman McLarty (a corporate lawyer), "blandly explained that P.C. 2685 was not supposed to be coercive".[60]

Early in 1940, the Mackenzie King state took a bolder step which showed its underlying attitude towards labour relations. By an order-in-council on January 11, the minister of justice arrested more than 100 trade union and labour activists, some Communists and some not, who were deemed to be a threat to "the safety of the State". C.S. Jackson, one of those arrested and imprisoned without trial for up to two years, had been attempting to organize workers at Canadian General Electric and Canadian Westinghouse plants. He recalled after the war:

> It was quite clear from my case, and that of many other union leaders, that the Canadian corporations, concerned about the rapid growth of unions, pressured a willing government to use the War Measures Act to try to stop the organizing drives.[61]

Kent Rowley, another labour organizer imprisoned under the regulations, later observed:

> King would not be the first politician who used the "patriotic effort" to rid himself of enemies. But in this case, it was clear that the War Measures Act was employed in a cowardly way to help the big money men behind King's party to clear their skirts of troublesome union organizers.[62]

Some of those "big money men" included the directors of U.S.

branch plants, whose head offices south of the border were highly experienced in union-busting. Like General Motors, the Ford Motor Company had a long history of anti-unionism couched in anti-communist rhetoric. Its branch plant, Ford of Canada, had become by wartime "a substantial force in the general industrial sector of the nation. As such, it was considered to be the leader in many areas by Canadian manufacturing interests; one of the most important had become labour relations."[63]

In April 1940, corporate and government co-operation came together in the creation of the Department of Munitions and Supply, headed by Clarence Decatur Howe. An entirely new division of government, this department quickly became the most singular and centralized organization in the history of the country, with its minister fully enjoying the opportunity to live up to his nickname, Clarence "Dictator" Howe, "Minister For Everything".[64]

Howe's Department of Munitions and Supply directed and co-ordinated all Canadian industry, including the building of new plants and the conversion of existing plants to war production. It filled all contracts for Canada's armed forces and many for the Allied military. Through Munitions and Supply, all production and use of raw materials were rigidly controlled and properly channelled. By 1943, Howe's department had become "one of the world's biggest business operations".[65] As *Canada In World War* II observes, "Canada was the only country [among the Allies] which handled all supply through a single agency".[66]

Grierson considered Howe's Department of Munitions and Supply to be an excellent example of what "corporate and co-operative energies" could accomplish. In a 1941 speech, he alluded to Howe's department as the "revolutionary centralization of financial, economic and even technocratic initiative in the State" through which "the dream of a free society" had been wisely discarded by statesmen (corporate and elected) and specialists.[67] There are several flattering references to Munitions and Supply in the wartime documentaries, though never is the audience informed that Howe's departmental advisors were provided by Chrysler, General Motors, General Electric, and Westinghouse, whose U.S. head offices had much to gain from this singular agency.[68] Similarly, both the wartime films and Grierson's speech failed to mention a few other details that Canadian audiences might have found enlightening at the time.

C.D. Howe and the branch-plant businessmen who commanded his extensive industrial empire were working in concert to make Canada more completely an economic colony of the United States. Throughout the war, "the integration of the industrial systems of Canada and the United States was immensely accelerated", with U.S. investment in Canada increased to $5.175 billion.[69] Simultaneously, Howe had jumped on the nuclear bandwagon, providing the top-secret Manhattan Project with access to Canada's entire uranium production from 1942 onwards.[70] The next step was perhaps inevitable: the 1944 construction of the first heavy-water reactor at Chalk River.

> Canada's chief scientific adviser, Chalmers Mackenzie, advised Howe that it was an unprecedented chance for Canada to 'get in on the ground floor' of a major new technological advance. 'It is an opportunity that Canada as a nation cannot afford to turn down,' he said. Howe needed no persuading: he saw the potential of a vast new industry....[71]

Later Howe created Atomic Energy of Canada, Ltd., with his friend Chalmers Mackenzie appointed as its head.

Whether or not Grierson, with access to Mackenzie King and his Cabinet, knew of the work on the atomic bomb or the construction at Chalk River, the wartime films seem to subtly prepare the populace for that "war machine beyond the wildest dreams of the Nazis" (*Tools of War*). Mass acceptance of the postwar nuclear agenda depended on a populace subservient to the wonders of modern science and the goals of the scientist-soldier ideal. In that sense, many of the wartime films certainly made their contribution, with their emphasis on the supremacy of technology and the need for an élite cadre of scientific experts to plan the postwar future.

With C.D. Howe and his U.S. branch-plant advisors co-ordinating the outlay of Canadian tax dollars and War Bond funding, there was a need for the proper co-ordination of labour. C.D. Howe, like his business colleagues, considered unions to be "a disruptive and potentially dangerous nuisance".[72] Not surprisingly, with Ford of Canada a leader in labour relations at the time, the situation for Canadian workers became increasingly worse as the Department of Munitions and Supply gained in efficiency and power.

In December 1940, Privy Council Order 7440 imposed a peculiar form of wage control on workers. "The new order directed the boards appointed under the Industrial Disputes Investigation Act to limit wage settlements to rates established during 1926–1929, a period of 'reasonable wage levels'. A cost-of-living bonus of $1.25 a week might be paid as an addition."[73] Desmond Morton refers to this new order as "a fresh weapon against unions and wage demands".[74] Ford of Canada was particularly skilled in using such a weapon. As George Burt recalled, "Ford had some really bad practices. They started you at seventy-five cents an hour. After six months you were entitled to an increase of ten cents. So they'd keep you for six months. Then they'd lay you off and rehire you again at seventy-five cents."[75]

Like many other corporate employers at the time, Ford was exploiting the patriotism of Canadian workers, who were willing to keep the wheels of industry moving for the war effort. Nevertheless, the attempts to gain union recognition continued. In 1941, at the Ford Windsor plant, the United Auto Workers (UAW) formally requested recognition from the company. According to David Moulton, "Wallace Campbell, the company president, refused the demand, stating his belief that the UAW did not represent the majority of plant employees at Ford. Instead, Campbell proposed the formation of a company union that would reach an agreement for the workers with the company."[76] Obviously, Mackenzie King's old solution to labour relations was still in favour among U.S. branch-plant directors in the absence of any legislation to outlaw company unions. After some "vigorous behind-the-scenes action", including intervention by the federal government, the UAW and Ford Windsor agreed to hold a recognition ballot, whose results established the UAW as the recognized bargaining agent at the plant. Nonetheless, as David Moulton writes, "The contract may have been signed, and the union established with stewards and committee men in the plants, but the company continued to make decisions as it had in the past, without regard to the men or the union."[77]

In their biography of C.D. Howe, Robert Bothwell and William Kilbourn note that early in the war American officials were sent north to study Canada's industrial relations. "They were surprised at what they found": a minister [Howe] "'closely allied to industry'", with many of his executives "'known to be antilabor'"; a minister of labour [McLarty] who was a corporation lawyer; and "'Canadian industrialists, especially in Toronto, [who] have preserved a strength and an arrogance surprising to an American.'"[78] This was the situation confronting the Canadian labour movement as war production moved towards its peak in 1943. It was also the context and the year in which Grierson's NFB established the industrial and trade union film circuits.

Major walkouts and disputes in Alberta, British Columbia, Ontario, and Quebec reflected labour's dissatisfaction with tight wage controls, double-digit inflation, corporate refusal to honour previously negotiated labour contracts, and the refusal of many employers to recognize unions.[79] In Ottawa, the federal Cabinet, at Mackenzie King's urging, asked the National War Labour Board to inquire into "labour relations and wage conditions in Canada". Hearings began in April 1943. Over the next two months, nearly every major trade union leader in the country appeared as a witness, as did dozens of government officials and business leaders. Labour's message was quite clear: wage control must be lifted for the lower-paid workers, with 55 cents an hour established as a rational basic wage rate, and a national labour code based on the Wagner Act must be drawn up.[80]

Some of the worst working conditions at the time were in Quebec, especially among employees for Dominion Textiles, a company which strongly fought the formation of a Canadian union. Madeleine Parent later recalled the wartime situation in Valleyfield:

> Wages went from 18 to 21 cents an hour for women and children to a high of 45-48, 50-53 cents for highly skilled loom-fixers and mechanics. Labour was cheap. There were no coffee breaks. At night the women and children worked ten hours with a break from midnight to one A.M. Men worked eleven or even up to twelve hours. This would mean that some men would go to work at six o'clock and come out at seven the next morning.... I remember seeing children of eleven or twelve years old coming off the night shift at midnight to go back to work at one o'clock.[81]

In the autumn of 1943, the National War Labour Board filed its minority and majority reports to Mackenzie King. The majority report, written by Mr. Justice C.P. McTague, recommended that Canada should have a labour code, as well as a system of family allowances to meet the demands of ill-paid workers.[82] The minority report, written by labour lawyer J.L. Cohen, backed the proposal for a national labour code but argued that wage controls on lower-paid workers should be removed and that a minimum wage of 50 cents an hour should be established.[83]

While these reports were being prepared throughout the summer of 1943, Grierson, in his role as director of the Wartime Information Board (WIB), was doing some information-gathering of his own. The

WIB had spent the summer conducting public-opinion polls on a number of issues, including views on "anti-inflation controls".[84] According to Grierson's interpretation of the survey findings, there was "'no considerable public demand for the abolition of the price and wage controls'", a poll result which he conveyed to Mackenzie King.[85]

The prime minister found both the majority and minority reports of the National War Labour Board "embarrassing".[86] Obviously, both McTague and Cohen were recommending measures, especially a labour code like the Wagner Act, that would displease Canadian and multinational business and assist the union movement. Mackenzie King decided to keep both reports secret. As Gary Evans notes, "Grierson's optimistic interpretation of Wartime Information Board surveys might have influenced him."[87] In Grierson's reading of the polling results, the public was in favour of the status quo and willing to sacrifice even more for the war effort.[88] Meanwhile, in his role as head of the NFB, he instituted measures to protect that status quo from the "selfish interests" of labour.

Financing for the NFB industrial film circuits came from government departments that were primarily concerned with production and labour: Munitions and Supply, the Wartime Prices and Trade Board, the Ministry of Labour, the National War Services.[89] The circuits were organized and administered by the NFB's Gordon Adamson, who also supervised 16mm production for the circuits in the first years. Wartime projectionist C.W. Gray noted that Adamson "worked in co-operation with boards of trade and chambers of commerce representing employer groups, and the sponsoring government departments".[90] This obvious alignment with management's concerns was further reflected in the trade union circuits, also administered by Adamson and organized shortly after the industrial circuits in 1943. "The agreement covering their operation was drafted when the Industrial Division of the National Film Board was only four months old. It was realized even then that the work would have to be carried on as a joint project between industrial and trade union showings."[91]

Sponsorship of the trade union circuits was provided by the NFB, the Workers' Education Association, the Canadian Congress of Labour, and the Trades and Labour Congress. By 1945, 300 union locals in 84 districts across Canada were involved in the circuit screenings. Selection of programming for the industrial circuits was made by Adamson in consultation with the sponsoring employer groups and government departments. Selection of films for the trade union circuits, which showed films after union meetings, was made by a central committee in Ottawa composed of Adamson, two other NFB representatives, and delegates from the Workers' Education Association, Canadian Congress of Labour, and the Trades and Labour Congress. Although this involvement between the NFB and labour organizations looks "progressive" at first glance, the content of the films raises questions.

With both the industrial and the union circuits tending, through their sponsorship, to reflect the interests of the employer, it is not surprising to find that their central concerns were worker morale and labour relations. Directive statesmanship in these areas was especially targetted at the unions. Ontario NFB representative Vaughn Deacon recalled: "We had showings right in the union halls of films of particular interest, information that the government felt the unions should have."[92] The nature of much of that information has been identified by Gary Evans: "The government was particularly keen to promote films encouraging formation of Labour Management Production Committees, which were in effect company unions."[93]

At least six films shown on the industrial and trade union circuits during the war advocated the formation of labour-management committees: *Our Film* (1942), *The Labour Front* (1943), *The New Pattern* (1944), *Democracy At Work* (1944), *Partners in Production* (1944), and *Labour Looks Ahead* (1945). *Our Film* and *Partners in Production* were imported from Great Britain; *The New Pattern* and *Democracy At Work* were compilation films made at the NFB using British-supplied footage. There may well have been several more of these imports, for as Vaughn Deacon has noted: "Many of the films in the trade union circuits were brought in from Britain."[94] An anecdote from C.W. Gray's text is also pertinent:

> One NFB representative serving trade unions in Toronto had some difficulty with films in the program that had been imported from Britain. He overcame the problem by introducing these films to his audiences, saying: "These films have a very strong English accent and you will have to listen very hard." After he instituted this practice he found that the commentary was far more easily understood and that local union members were much more likely to involve themselves in a discussion following the showing.[95]

Of the films dealing specifically with Canada, *The Labour Front* speaks of "progressive plants" where "management and labour cooperation" is evident. *Labour Looks Ahead* explores the extent to which labour had been co-operating with corporate employers and government throughout the war. The film, made in 1945, refers to "the 300 Labour-Management Production Committees" that had been successfully formed thus far. It would be interesting to know to what extent those 300 "company unions" overlapped with the 300 union locals served by the wartime NFB circuits. Whatever the case, the wartime NFB, under Grierson's tutelage, was advocating the very "solution" to labour relations that the U.S. branch plants (especially Ford of Canada) had been extolling. Such labour-management committees were an obvious throw-back to Mackenzie King's work for the Rockefeller Foundation.

In *Industry and Humanity,* Mackenzie King compared his Industrial Representation Plan (the Rockefeller Plan) of 1915 with a very similar plan developed in Great Britain two years later and based on the Whitley Report. Insisting that each plan "was in no way connected with the other", he wrote that "both owe their origin to ideas that were 'in the air'".[96] Thus, capital on both sides of the Atlantic adopted similar means for co-opting labour through variously named labour-management committees. If it was a solution in the air, Mackenzie King traced it directly to its source in World War I:

> Confronted with the necessity of vastly increasing output, all classes have been compelled to recognize the great importance of Labor's part in production. Assent to methods of highest efficiency involved on the part of Labor a surrender of restrictive devices by which through the past Labor has sought to fortify itself against the exclusive control of Capital and Management.[97]

In other words, because of British labour's patriotic effort in World War I ("the necessity of vastly increasing output"), labour surrendered unionism ("restrictive devices") in exchange for something else. "To win Labor's acquiescence, the Government [in Great Britain] ... found it imperative to extend to Labor something of that participation in control of policy which underlies partnership."[98]

Mackenzie King must have expected something similar to happen in Canada during World War II. The patriotism of working people would in itself curtail the union movement, which may explain why the Canadian Congress of Labour and the Trades and Labour Congress sponsored wartime NFB circuits advocating "company unions"—an effort to show good faith. But Mackenzie King was not about to make the same mistake that had occurred in Canada during and after World War I, when the government had failed to gain the consent of labour. Unlike the British government at the time, the Canadian government had made no effort to transform the patience of labour's patriotism during the war into an effective partnership afterwards, and the labour situation in the country had exploded in such messy imbroglios as the Winnipeg General Strike and a series of militant actions across the country. Sir Robert Borden's administration seemed to know little about "the manufacture of consent". Mackenzie King, on the other hand, was well informed and well advised.

In *Industry and Humanity,* Mackenzie King made note of one particular detail mentioned in the British Whitley Report: "the great majority of the causes of industrial unrest ... have their root in certain psychological conditions", especially "the feeling in the minds of the workers that their conditions of work and destinies are being determined by a distant authority over which they have no influence...."[99] It was this feeling that the British industrial councils (the equivalent to Mackenzie King's labour-management conciliation boards) were intended to address, without actually changing the economic structure in which such "distant authority" ruled. Corporate and state films extolling the nobility of the worker were another way of addressing those "psychological conditions" and feelings that might lead to unrest. Thus, by the 1930s in England, effective measures for co-opting the labour union movement had been underway. Wartime Canada still had some catching up to do in the creation of consent.

The extent to which the wartime NFB's advocacy of company unions influenced workers' opinion of the Canadian union movement or helped delay legislation to improve union and worker status in Canada is difficult to assess. Perhaps that is something that only members of the union movement themselves might accurately determine. In any case there were more than 66 NFB travelling projectionists serving the industrial and trade union circuits. Their monthly slate of films reportedly reached 300 union locals in 84 districts across Canada, and 385,000 factory workers every month.[100] This "company union" advocacy further reveals the paternalistic politics of Grierson, who in 1941 clearly stated his position that given the conditions of modern technocracy, the ideal of workers' self-management was unpractical and inefficient.[101]

All the NFB wartime non-theatrical circuits relied heavily on films imported from Great Britain and the United States. This was especially the case with the rural circuits, with their evening program length of 90 minutes. As C.W. Gray writes:

> Despite the fact that when the NFB rural circuits commenced operation the Board had only been producing films for a little over two years, it was remarkable that in this short period of time a backlog of 40 or 50 films, excellent, for their purpose, had been built up. Nevertheless, it was still necessary to go outside of Canada and purchase other films to provide a good variety in the program.[102]

Virtually one-half of the films listed in the NFB's 1943 film catalogue (46 out of 102 titles) were imported from Great Britain or the United States, and that listing does not include the many shorts and series brought in especially for showing on the rural circuits. According to Gray, "While the film programs were selected at the national level, they were distributed through provincial agents.... Rural schools and community groups usually took advantage of the opportunity each month to bring in other films for use in classrooms, and to supplement the evening program...."[103] Projectionist recall and available documentation reveal that the rural circuit programming regularly included the "Why We Fight" series from the United States, Walt Disney cartoons and campaign shorts, the U.S. armed services comedy series "Snafu", short films featuring actors like Bing Crosby, American Red Cross safety and health films, animation films from Great Britain, U.S. Department of Labor films, and Charlie Chaplin comedies.[104] It is tempting to see these imports in Griersonian terms. As he wrote in his film policy recommendations for the Canadian government, "What is the difference whether a film comes from Hollywood or Timbuktu or Saskatoon so long as it is about the life of man as it is lived and dreamed in common everywhere?"[105] But C.W. Gray provides a different explanation of the primary consideration behind the importation of films: national programmers for the rural circuits had to import films "to provide a good variety in the film program".

The primary emphasis in filmmaking at the wartime NFB was the making of films about work, about international geopolitics, films focussing on "the moods of resolution" that Grierson considered so necessary to stress the urgency of duty, sacrifice, total effort. Thus, the Canadian content for the rural circuits focussed on civic duty and allegiance to central authority, with insistent voice-overs urging the viewers on to greater effort in total war. But no audience can endure 90 minutes of this. C.W. Gray's circuit diary for the years 1942 and 1943 resounds with audience requests for relief from the barrage of state propaganda: "A brief comedy would please the children"; "Would it be possible to have a cartoon next time?"; "A cartoon would have been very well appreciated"; "A suitable cartoon would enhance interest"; "We still think a short comic at the last would help."[106] Though the circuits eventually incorporated the NFB's "Chants Populaires / Community Sing" series, as well as other NFB animations (notably the work of Norman McLaren), it is evident that the primary way of providing balance and variety in the circuit programming was through the use of films made elsewhere. This policy had important long-term effects.

The use of American cartoons, comedies, shorts, and series—with their Hollywood entertainment values, popular stars, comic relief, and less insistent tone ("Why We Fight" vs. "Canada Carries On" and "World in Action")—subtly reinforced a significant split in audience attitudes, a split in which Canadian content became associated with documentary, propaganda, "moods of resolution", central authority, and American content became associated with entertainment, comedy, "moods of relaxation": relief from Canadian content itself. Once the war was over, Canadian audiences may well have retained these expectations, looking to media from south of the border to fulfil their entertainment needs.

At the start of the wartime circuits, many in the rural audiences had never seen a sound-film before, and some had never seen a film. Most of the rural communities did not even have electricity, so that the majority of the travelling projectionists hired by the NFB had to carry gasoline-powered motor generators to run their 16mm projectors. Initially then, the circuit audiences would have had no specific expectations regarding Canadian films. By having the wartime NFB focus on "the moods of resolution", while at the same time importing films from outside the country to meet the "moods of relaxation", Grierson helped to divide the country's expectations along an axis that actually served the U.S. entertainment industry structure.

By the end of the war, rural audiences were asking for feature-length entertainment, as Gray's diary notes: "For a showing of this type, a longer entertainment feature should be included"; "Stressing entertainment features will be more effective"; "We would like full feature film entertainment."[107] As a result of the film commissioner's policy recommendation to the Canadian government, however, support for an indigenous feature film industry was effectively delayed. Indeed, Grierson's admired colleague, C.D. Howe, was instrumental in getting the infamous Canadian Co-operation Project underway in postwar years.[108]

The NFB's wartime rural circuits, under Grierson's tutelage, set a pattern that was decisive for Canada's media future, especially television. The continuing demands of the Canadian audience for ready access to American entertainment via cable, satellite-dish, super-stations, and pay-TV are, in a sense, the true legacy of the wartime rural circuits. Not only was the split in audience expectations created, or at least enforced, but the Canadian state itself had established a precedent of making Hollywood entertainment readily available across the Canadian hinterland. That precedent was a quantum leap beyond a simple non-interference with the distribution–exhibition structure as it operated in urban movie theatres controlled by the Hollywood majors. Having itself expanded the Canadian audience for American product, state policy has ever since remained aligned with the desires of the MPAA lobby.

9

The Inevitable Denouement

In the last year of the war, Grierson had reached the peak of his career, advising the governments of at least three countries—the United States, Britain, and Canada—on their postwar media needs, running his London Film Centre, which was rivalling the Crown Film Unit in its influence and output, and overseeing the Canadian NFB, which had grown into an institution of considerable size, with more than 600 employees. Like an expert juggler, Grierson was keeping all these balls in motion, preventing whatever contradictory or competing factors were involved from interfering in his extraordinary display of competence.

By the spring of 1945, Grierson was in Washington, helping the State Department prepare a documentary film and giving advice on the role of documentary in postwar public relations.[1] On April 14, 1945, Al Sherman's Washington column in *Boxoffice* magazine reported "Grierson To Head State Department Film Unit":

> [Grierson] is slated to take over active operation of a film unit sponsored by the State Department, with Assistant Secretary Archibald MacLeish actively supervising.... It is believed that if the State Department wins full approval of such a program, (to explain American foreign policy)

> Grierson will assume active control of all productions. Grierson has been consulted at previous times by the American Government on documentary film production....[2]

The story was picked up by the *Globe and Mail* in its April 19 and 20 editions.[3] In the wake of this media leak, Grierson returned immediately to Ottawa. The minister responsible for the NFB, J.J. McCann, issued an official denial of the rumour: "There was no foundation for the earlier report that Mr. Grierson was resigning his government post here to take a position with the United States government on film work."[4] Whatever was taking place behind the scenes, this official denial diverted attention from the issue for the time being. In one important circle of influence, however, the rumour raised considerable concern.

In the labyrinthine brain-pan of J. Edgar Hoover, director of the FBI, the rumour twigged a synaptical connection that was not about to be disengaged by a simple disavowal from a Canadian spokesman. In 1942, the FBI had opened a file on Grierson, though it contained only two items until 1945: an unidentified informant's suspicion that Grierson was "a definite communistic sympathizer" and a movie column by John T. McManus in *P.M.* magazine commenting on the NFB film *Inside Fighting Russia*.[5] Never one to be dissuaded by such flimsy "evidence", Hoover latched onto the rumoured State Department offer to Grierson with the tenacity of a pit bull, and contacted the U.S. embassy in London on May 24, 1945, for background information on Grierson:

> From information appearing in Bureau files, it is indicated that John Grierson is Communisticly inclined and that several of the films he has produced in Canada appear to be written and directed from a pro-Soviet viewpoint.[6]

With the FBI director on his trail, Grierson's juggling act was about to fall apart.

The most succinct statement of Grierson's politics, expressed in his own words, is this 1942 quotation:

> The armies of the world are carving out new geographical concepts and shapes. The processes of total war are developing new economic concepts, and more modern methods of administrative control. First things are miraculously coming first, including the food and faith of the people.

> Though minor social changes are not major political ones and the radish may be one colour outside and another in, the present flow of social decency must lubricate the development of state planning, corporate thinking and co-operative citizenship. The most important of the British films have, of course, been those which have seized on one or other of these changes, and it is of first-rate significance that Jack Beddington should have sponsored them.[7]

This tangle of rhetoric, innuendo, and allusion—which I would not attempt to decipher here without the past eight chapters to buttress my interpretation—illuminates Grierson's tragic flaw. That flaw was *not* that behind the rhetoric he advocated "minor social changes" rather than "major political ones", or that Jack Beddington's Shell–Mex BP remained his preferred documentary sponsor, or even that he was ideologically aligned with those "new economic concepts and more modern methods of administrative control" which favoured the emergent multinationals. The flaw, rather, is hinted at in Grierson's own words: "the radish may be one colour outside and another in."

From the late 1920s onwards, Grierson had adopted a persona and a style of rhetoric which were both persuasive and vague. His biographer implies that no one ever really knew Grierson, that his "privacy was inviolable", and that he enjoyed being enigmatic, "unpredictable", the charismatic, but undecipherable, centre of action.[8] As Irving Jacoby assessed Grierson's "complex character":

> He played at being a film pundit, a political thinker, a social gambler, a tough journalist. He would sometimes think of himself as a show-biz character, or a modern radical philosopher, or a Jew or a member of the Mafia....[9]

Along with what Jacoby calls "disguises", Grierson was an accomplished master of rhetoric who well knew his verbal powers of persuasion. As he wrote to Stephen Tallents from Australia in 1940:

> I know what will happen when I get down to planning the siting of this curious little act of ours in Australia. I shall as usual have to relate it, not to the real objective needs of Australia, which are, as anywhere else, human management, responsibility, illumination, and humility before the Lord; but to the felt needs which, I can lay a million to one now, will turn out to be sectional, selfish, political, vulgar and dishonest. Nevertheless, I shall relate the process to these very needs ... I shall discuss with consummate

> ease the needs for focussing the popular mind on the national purpose, and away from what it may now consider its immediate interest; and each dark mind will leap to a vision of its own, thereby, advantage.[10]

Presumably, the "advantage" the Imperial Relations Trust stood to gain through the powers of Griersonian rhetoric was in the "Empire integrations and so forth" which a British propaganda base in Australia, like the one in Canada, might achieve, although within the same passage Grierson also writes of some "seed of conversion" which was "vouchsafed to us to administer".[11]

Grierson's internationalist rhetoric was purposely vague enough to be interpreted by his listeners—including his filmmaking colleagues, his multinational sponsors, his government sponsors, and his Canadian disciples—according to their own agendas. This profound ability to use rhetoric in a way that "each dark mind will leap to a vision of its own" fully rebounded on Grierson in the postwar years. If, as Grierson's own metaphor of the radish suggests, he had all along been pink on the outside and "another colour inside", J. Edgar Hoover had neither the wit nor the intelligence to follow the intricacies of Grierson's purposely enigmatic manoeuverings. Hoover's own "dark mind" seized on the mirroring vagueness of Grierson's internationalist rhetoric and leapt to a "vision of its own"—the inevitable vision that any 1940s FBI mind would leap to. Ironically, the very man who had worked for multinational capitalism's next, "progressive" stage, found himself hounded and harassed as an enemy of those interests.

But there may have been another factor at work in the postwar curtailment of Grierson's career. In the immediate years following World War II, not even J. Edgar Hoover was the ultimate arbitrator on the U.S. political scene.

While the FBI was quietly making attempts to fill out its meagre dossier on Grierson in the summer of 1945, World War II was coming to a close. Grierson, always ready for new challenges, resigned from the NFB on August 7, effective three months later. He began organizing the non-profit International Film Associates Inc. in Ottawa and Washington, lining up research and survey work to be done for UNRRA (United Nations Relief and Rehabilitation Administration) and for corporate sponsors such as the Hudson's Bay Company.[12] But then, on September 6, 1945, Igor Gouzenko, a cypher clerk in the Soviet embassy in Ottawa, decided to defect to the West and turned himself over to Canadian authorities with information about a Soviet spy ring operating in

Canada. By October, the RCMP was investigating the validity of Gouzenko's allegations. Life for Grierson would never be the same again.

The bundle of files that Gouzenko handed over to the Canadian authorities "proved beyond doubt" that the Soviet embassy had been the base for a very active spy ring.[13]

> Its tentacles were found to extend into the cipher section of the Department of External Affairs, the National Research Council, the Wartime Information Board, the British High Commission, the group of scientists from Britain who were pursuing atomic research in Montreal, and the House of Commons (the country's one Communist MP was in due course sentenced to a term of imprisonment for espionage). Mackenzie King, in spite of his long-standing distrust of Russia, was at first unwilling to believe Gouzenko's story and only gradually came to admit that Canada's ally had been carrying on these activities against her during the war.[14]

Mackenzie King did not perceive the Gouzenko affair as something entirely related to atomic espionage. He wrote in his diary, "It is of course all part of a world revolution—a world communist movement to get on the part of workers a control of the government completely out of the hands of those who have privilege, power, etc."[15]

Among the material produced by Gouzenko was a notebook containing an entry made by the assistant military attaché at the Soviet embassy in Ottawa: "'Research Council—report on the organisation and work. Freda to the professor through Grierson'".[16] "Freda" was alleged to be Freda Linton, who had been Grierson's secretary at the NFB from May to September 1944, and who was said to have been a contact within the spy ring. "The professor" was apparently Raymond Boyer, an alleged Soviet agent working in the National Research Council.[17] Gouzenko told the Canadian authorities "that the work Freda Linton was doing at the Film Board was unsatisfactory to Moscow. They wanted her placed in a more important department, the National Research Council ... and suggested that Grierson's influence should be used to get her into this position."[18]

A royal commission to investigate the Gouzenko allegations was appointed by order-in-council on February 5, 1946, with Robert Taschereau and R.L. Kellock appointed as judges.[19] At the commission hearings, Gouzenko was asked, "But was Grierson an agent?", to which he responded, "Oh no, Grierson is not an agent, but the idea was to get Freda in the position where she could get a more important position in the organization [the National Research Council] through the influence of Grierson".[20] Freda Linton had at one time decided to try to recruit Grierson as a Soviet spy. The response from Moscow was succinct: "stay away from Grierson".[21]

As Kirwan Cox writes in "The Grierson Files", "The Freda Linton episode was the only 'evidence' the FBI ever uncovered that seemed to incriminate Grierson as a Communist or a spy."[22] It was flimsy evidence, but the "dark mind" of the FBI concluded that Moscow's directive to "stay away from Grierson" meant Grierson was already a Communist spy.[23]

The Taschereau–Kellock Commission turned up nothing to implicate Grierson, though his philosophical responses to the Commission's questions may have been somewhat exasperating. For example:

> Q. Would you say then that the effect of all that is that you are not a member of the Communist party?
>
> A. Oh no.
>
> Q. That is officially. What would you say about subscribing to any of their views? Would you say that your inclinations were of the leftist variety ... ?
>
> A. Not at all; I do not think that way. I am entirely a person who is concerned with the establishment of good international understanding. Therefore I am concerned with the floating of all ideas. I mean, I get as much from Gobineau* as I get from Marx.[24]

When asked about the political atmosphere at the NFB, Grierson characterized it as "progressive, not leftist, thought"—a significant distinction.[25]

Thus, there was really no evidence that Grierson was either a Communist or a Soviet agent. I think this was probably known within important circles of power in the United States, but the cloud of suspicion could be a useful mechanism in the Cold War milieu. One of the most important issues in the postwar United States was the free flow of information, an issue central not only to the Department of State but also to U.S. plans for the United Nations. It is at least feasible that Grierson's demise hinged less on the issue of Communism than on the

* Joseph Arthur de Gobineau was an anti-semitic ideologue who influenced the philosophy of the Third Reich.

issue of the free flow of information. When he proved unwilling to abide by U.S. plans in the latter arena, Grierson could be conveniently dismissed on the basis of FBI files.

In the spring of 1946, Grierson was being seriously considered for a job at the United Nations, as Assistant to the Secretary General of the UN in charge of Press Relations.[26] As Collier and Horowitz have documented, one of the key driving forces behind the formation of the UN was the Rockefeller family, who donated the land, helped decide (through the State Department via Junior's son, Nelson) which countries were to be included as founding members, and tended to view this new world body as primarily the result of Rockefeller initiative.[27]

Although Grierson's expertise in media matters made him an obvious contender for the UN position, no doubt his Rockefeller contacts helped. Grierson had advised the Foundation on film and public opinion in the 1920s, and had courted sponsorship from Beddington's Shell–Mex BP (the cartel including Standard Oil) from 1934 onwards; his colleague Paul Rotha had visited the United States in September 1937 on invitation from the Rockefeller Foundation and the Rockefeller-endowed Museum of Modern Art film library.[28] In 1940 Grierson and Rotha's London Film Centre had secured Foundation funding for efforts including publication of the *Documentary News Letter*. In autumn 1945, Grierson again gained funding from the Rockefeller Foundation for his World Today Inc., which he officially incorporated on March 20, 1946.[29]

Following Grierson's first appearance before the Taschereau–Kellock Commission in April 1946, J. Edgar Hoover was so convinced that Grierson was a "Communistic sympathizer" that he "sent out Grierson's dossier to various senior bureaucrats in Washington".[30] He was so concerned that, according to Kirwan Cox, he wrote to President Truman on April 16 making specific reference to the fact that Grierson was being considered for the UN post.[31] Though Hoover's FBI was adamant that Grierson not get the UN post and was doing its utmost to cause problems and delays in Grierson's securing of an immigration visa, it is not all that clear that other U.S. organizations and powers believed the flimsy evidence that Hoover was circulating about Grierson.

According to Forsyth Hardy, in the months following the Taschereau–Kellock Commission in 1946, Grierson was approached by at least two of the most important media institutions in the United States. The MPAA lobby was "impressed by what he had achieved in

Canada" and was interested in employing his services, and William S. Paley, president of the board of CBS, was negotiating "a proposal that Grierson should be head of C.B.S. News".[32] These approaches would hardly have been made if the prevailing view was that Grierson was guilty of "Communistic sympathies". Indeed, according to Hardy, Grierson in late 1946 was advising the president's Committee for Financing Foreign Trade.[33] Although J. Edgar Hoover ordered a full, secret investigation of Grierson as of September 12, 1946—an investigation that involved tremendous personal harassment for both Grierson and his friends—it does not appear as though others in power in the U.S. were convinced that Grierson was a Communist.[34] It is at least feasible that Grierson did not get the UN post because of another issue.

The United States emerged from World War II virtually unscathed and with its technostructure of corporate, governmental, military, and media interests fully co-ordinated for an expansionist effort of global proportions. Central to that expansion was the elimination of "artificial barriers" to U.S. media interests, which would pave the way for the global markets so necessary to multinational capitalism. By February 1946, the State Department had made public its plan "to do everything within its power along political or diplomatic lines to help break down the artificial barriers to the expansion of private American news agencies, magazines, motion pictures, and other media of communications throughout the world".[35] This expansionist plan was couched in the modernist language of consent: "Freedom of the press—and freedom of exchange of information generally—is an integral part of our foreign policy."[36] But there were some media experts at the time who were quite capable of seeing past the rhetoric to the political issues involved.

The free flow of information was a central issue behind the scenes at the fledgling UN and a key focus of the first General Conference of UNESCO in November 1946.[37] At the time, Grierson was also being considered for the post of director of mass communications for UNESCO, and he made his presence felt at that first General Conference. Grierson joined the British delegation examining the UNESCO section on mass communications, which had been drafted by William Farr, René Maheu, and Philippe Desjardins. The British delegation included David Hardman, J.B. Priestley, Ritchie Calder, Grierson, Edgar Anstey, Helen de Mouilpied, Jacquetta Hawkes, A.D. Ritchie, Paul Rotha, and Basil Wright.[38] According to Hardy, "The British experts, led by Grierson, tore the draft to pieces", and were told by the Belgian chairman of the conference, Jan Kuypers, to go away and redraft the mass communications section.[39]

In 1944, Grierson had advised the Canadian government to forgo any postwar plans for a commercial film industry and to avoid interfering with the Hollywood distribution-exhibition structure in Canada. His argument was couched in terms that were obviously aligned with both State Department and MPAA designs for postwar media expansion. But at the same time, he was advising the British government to take a more radical approach, through the regulation of private companies (the Hollywood-based distribution-exhibition sector in England), in order to ensure that British-made films gained access to greater distribution, both domestically and world-wide. This contradiction suggests that Grierson, ever the Empire man, felt that the film aspirations of a country like Canada were simply muddying the picture, whereas Britain was obviously entitled to "a truly national film industry". When the UN was debating the issue of the free flow of information in 1946, Grierson made his position clear to the UNESCO conference:

> We must at any cost encourage mutual understanding between nations, which pre-supposes that each can speak not only to its neighbour but to all countries in the world. We must work to remove all barriers to the free circulation of information. It must be a two-way traffic, and information must be carried from one country to another and from all countries to any one country for the sake of normal and mutual understanding between all.[40]

Although there is some characteristic Griersonian ambiguity here, especially in the call "to remove all barriers to the free circulation of information", his position was at variance with that of the U.S. State Department and corporate interests, which were not particularly interested in "two-way traffic". It certainly seems possible that Grierson, in taking this stance, nettled the American powers-that-be. They had been accustomed to a Canadian film commissioner who during the war had fully catered to Hollywood interests and to a Rockefeller-funded documentarian who had always espoused the international line. I think it was at this point and on this issue that Grierson's dismissal from the United States was decided. Certainly the issue came to a head in subsequent months.

On January 15, 1947, Julian Huxley, director general of UNESCO, offered Grierson the mass communications post with the organization, which Grierson accepted on January 20.[41] J. Edgar Hoover was furious because his efforts to keep Grierson out of the United States were now frustrated by Grierson's immunity as a UN official.[42] Nevertheless, Hoover's hounding continued and Grierson's tenure at the UN was cut short. By February 1, 1948, he was "dismissed" as an employee of UNESCO, apparently because of FBI information that he was a "possible subversive".[43] But in later years, Grierson provided this aspect of the story:

> I had a very particular responsibility at UNESCO at the time. I was in Mass Communications. I was only there for one purpose and one purpose only: to watch this situation of the "free flow of information" in relation to UNESCO. The Americans thought of taking over, of financing, UNESCO and taking over all the radio stations, which had been set up by the great warring nations, and putting a radio network around the world.... I was approached as the guy who was going to be the key in this great World Radio Network, and in the preaching of peace throughout the world. The money, of course, was so vast that the budget of Mass Communications of UNESCO would have been eight times the size of the whole of the rest of UNESCO. So, this totally excellent scheme was offered to me. You talk about somebody being taken up to the heights and tested there. The character was taken up—that was me. All these domains should be mine. Well, I've been there and this is against my principles in some fundamental way.... We were handing over this vast machine to American know-how, to American technicians, to an inevitable American stranglehold on information.[44]

It seems that if Grierson had been willing to go along with the American plan and with the State Department's implicit definition of "the free flow of information", Hoover's virulent opposition to Grierson would have been kept in check by the more important powers of statecraft at the time. But as things turned out, Grierson's dismissal could be handily couched in terms suitable to the Cold War.

Although it is possible to admire Grierson's courage under duress in these events, his decision on the American plan, and his strength and obvious talent in many areas, he was to a great extent the architect of his own postwar difficulties. There was a reason why he was "approached as the guy who was going to be the key" to U.S. postwar media expansion. His actions, policy, and rhetoric throughout his tenure as Canada's film commissioner led U.S. interests to assume that he was entirely on-side in their postwar media agenda. They could not have known, until the free flow of information issue fully surfaced in autumn of 1946, that Grierson hoped to carve out a greater niche for the British documentary movement in the postwar world.

If the oil cartel of Beddington's Shell–Mex BP was the model for much of Grierson's thinking—with its harmonious co-ordination of formerly competing interests, its international alignment of British and U.S. multinationals, its "progressive" potential for peace-time improvements—then that model could be also applied to Grierson's dream for the British documentary movement. Just as in the 1930s Standard Oil had come to recognize Shell and British Petroleum as equal partners, who might co-operate to control production and keep other companies in check, so the United States and Britain might co-operate in the postwar media scene. But that meant that the U.S. monopoly over the world screen market would have to give way to British desires, especially the desire of the British documentarians to have their films reach a world market.

In his efforts to achieve that end, Grierson had tried to juggle too many competing interests and contradictory political positions, never dreaming that they would all collapse at his feet in the single-minded milieu of postwar American planning. He had played a dangerous rhetorical game, "one colour outside and another in", not recognizing that it would backfire, with betrayals felt on several sides and his own brilliant career curtailed. Perhaps, in that sense, he really was "an innocent abroad".

Conclusion

The Hurricane of Change

It is also fairly plain what areas of chaos have to be reduced to order, whatever political alignment develops.

JOHN GRIERSON, 1942

In Grierson's chosen profession of "mind-bending" (his term),[1] his greatest concern was order and his greatest fear the disorder or chaos that might result from individualism, from liberal democracy, from economic nationalism, from people thinking for themselves in their own "amateur" ways. This prevailing theme, order versus chaos, runs through much of his prewar and wartime work and became the basis for his totalitarian stance during the war years in Canada.

When reading Grierson's published writings and speeches from that period it is easy to forget, because of the simplified and inspirational rhetoric, that the author was a highly informed and educated political scientist who read several newspapers every day and who was operating within the highest levels of corporate and state power. For example, in a 1941 pamphlet published by the Canadian Association for Adult Education, Grierson urged educators:

> Go out and ask men to mobilize themselves for the destruction of greed and selfishness. And mean it. Ask them to forget their personal dreams and pleasures and deny themselves for the obliteration of economic anarchy and disorder all over the world. And mean it.... Say with the Prime Minister of Canada that 'never again in our own land or in any other land

> will the gods of material power, of worldly possession and of special privilege be permitted to exercise their sway'.[2]

With U.S. multinational branch plants advising the government on both industrial relations and the wartime reconstruction of Canada, it stretches the imagination to assume that either Mackenzie King or Grierson was uninformed about the ways in which those powers of "special privilege" were exercising their sway. Rather, the rhetoric can be placed within the context of Mackenzie King's model of the four partners in industry: capital, management, labour, and the community. The first two partners were proceeding quite handsomely during the war. Labour and the community, however, needed some professional "mind-bending" so that consent, and not chaos, might be the order of the day.

Gary Evans observes:

> If one ignores the subjective connotation usually applied to the word 'totalitarian', that is what governments had become during the national emergency. They had used wartime to develop powers to manipulate the major media to reach every level of society for their own particular ends in order to win the war. Grierson had wanted to extend those powers into peacetime. Liberal democracy said no.[3]

Evans's last sentence here is debatable. It's evident that World War II was a turning point for multinational capitalism and for democracy itself. The exigencies of war provided both the means and the justification for the maturation of an immense technostructure poised to launch multinational business into its greatest period of global expansion. The co-ordination of corporate and state powers, most tellingly exemplified in the top-secret, transnational Manhattan Project, was not about to be dismantled after the war. Similarly, those same "Fraternity" members who had traded with the enemy throughout the war were positioned to expand into global markets created in the post-war period by the expansion of U.S. media according to "the free flow of information".

Grierson recognized that this expansion was on the postwar horizon, and he seemed to have hoped that England, and the British documentary movement, might remain significant players within the new world order. What he may not have fully perceived, at least until after the war, was that U.S. interests had fully taken to heart the prediction of media magnate Henry Luce: that this was to be "the American Century".

Within that goal, a colonized Canada—rich in natural resources and without identified and boundaried self-interest—would become (and remain) the model for "international co-operation", the greatest "friend" and trading partner of the United States, and the most lucrative market for a key sector of the U.S. multinational economy: information.

Fully marginalized in the media world, unable even to "Canadianize" its own airwaves or its movie and TV screens, the country and its policy-makers have dutifully followed for the last 50 years the "internationalist" advice of the legendary media expert, refusing to tamper with an industry structure that ensures that the market share for Canadian media *inside Canada* remains miniscule. As Susan Crean writes:

> The figures tell the tale: three to five per cent of the screen time in Canadian movie houses is devoted to Canadian films; two to four per cent of videocassettes sold are Canadian, twenty per cent of books sold are published by Canadian-owned firms which publish eighty per cent of the Canadian-authored titles; ninety-seven per cent of film revenues leave the country, ninety-five per cent headed for the U.S.; eighty-five per cent of records and tapes sold in Canada are non-Canadian; seventy-seven per cent of the magazines sold are foreign; ninety-five per cent of the drama aired on television is non-Canadian.[4]

This, too, is part of the legacy of Griersonian internationalism as he preached it during his wartime tenure.

In this sense, Grierson was a significant part of that hurricane of change in which Canada was fully caught up during World War II, undergoing an industrial transformation that might otherwise have taken some 50 to 75 years. The colonizing interests directing that transformation, aided and abetted by the Mackenzie King state, would proceed to wreak a similar transformation on much of the postwar world, especially within those Third World countries whose governments had been successfully courted and propped up by U.S. interests.

Grierson's thinking was aligned with those multinational interests; he saw them as a possible way of bringing peace, global harmony, and economic order into a potentially chaotic and disordered global situation. So strongly did he believe in the potential within "corporate and co-operative" or mass society that he became admittedly totalitarian in his effort. Gary Evans notes that Grierson and Legg were conducting "a war for men's minds, a propaganda war which employed the new techniques of mass persuasion that had been learned in the First World War.

Not surprisingly, they were the same techniques which were used by the fascist enemies who hated democracy and who believed might determined what was right."[5]

It is a truism within depth psychology that, without consciousness, people become similar to the very enemy they despise and attempt to eliminate. Grierson believed that it was possible to be "totalitarian for good" and failed to recognize that not only does the end not justify the means, but the means actually determine the end. In the intervening years since World War II, there has been the rise of what Bertram Gross has termed "friendly fascism": the increasingly totalitarian collusion of big business and big government via the corporate state, in order to "manage" society in the interests of the rich and powerful.[6] This "new face of power" functions according to the rationalization of a global economy through multinational business (that is, beyond national politics), through mass subservience to oligarchic and technocratic authority, and through the control and shaping of information and media spectacle for the consent of the governed. In these terms, Grierson was an early advocate of this new order, which had surfaced during the first decades of the century but which fully emerged in the immediate aftermath of World War II. His expert public-relations advice to Jack Beddington's Shell–Mex BP oil cartel paid off after the war. As his filmmaking colleagues Edgar and Daphne Anstey have written:

> In the immediate postwar years, Shell and other oil companies established film units in Iran, Iraq, Venezuela, and Singapore. Most were staffed by Grierson-trained personnel. In Venezuela, Shell used film as a principal means of promoting an officially adopted policy of using oil revenue to diversify industry and provide modern social services. It was not so much Grierson's teaching that produced this unexpected enlightenment as the fact that he trained his filmmakers to bring to the level of full consciousness what might be called the hidden logic of history.[7]

For Grierson, that "hidden logic" involved the full maturation of multinational capitalism into its most "progressive" stage. Through the release of corporate and mass energies, combined with full mechanization and technocratic planning, order would prevail across the planet. It was, he said, "what people in their hearts have been harking for" as the fulfillment of an era. Those who felt differently were obviously the dupe of their own amateur judgements and clearly "rotted in the old, untotal ways".

Notes

Introduction

1 Elizabeth Sussex, *The Rise and Fall of British Documentary: The Story of the Film Movement Founded by John Grierson* (Berkeley: University of California Press, 1975), p. 209.

2 Ibid.

3 Ibid.

4 Forsyth Hardy, ed., *Grierson On Documentary* (London: Faber & Faber, 1946), p. 117.

5 Forsyth Hardy, *John Grierson: A Documentary Biography* (London: Faber & Faber, 1979), p. 258.

6 Jack Ellis, "John Grierson's Relation with British Documentary During World War Two," in The John Grierson Project–McGill University, eds., *John Grierson and the* NFB (Toronto: ECW Press, 1984), p. 63.

Chapter One: Simple Twists of Fate

1 Forsyth Hardy, *John Grierson: A Documentary Biography* (London: Faber & Faber, 1979), p. 30.

2 Ibid., p. 31.

3 Quoted in George S. McGovern and Leonard F. Guttridge, *The Great Coalfield War* (Boston: Houghton Mifflin, 1972), p. 294.

4 Peter Collier and David Horowitz, *The Rockefellers: An American Dynasty* (New York: Holt, Rinehart and Winston, 1976), pp. 100–101.

5 McGovern and Guttridge, *Coalfield War,* p. 294.

6 Quoted in Milton Moskowitz, Michael Katz, and Robert Levering, eds., *Everybody's Business: An Almanac* (San Francisco: Harper & Row, 1980), p. 532.

7 Ibid., p. 533.

8 Quoted in ibid.

9 Quoted in McGovern and Guttridge, *Coalfield War,* p. 294.

10 Ibid., p. 297.

11 Quoted in ibid.

12 Ibid.

13 C.P. Stacey, *A Very Double Life* (Halifax: Formac / Goodread Biographies, 1976), p. 21.

14 McGovern and Guttridge, *Coalfield War,* p. 294.

15 Quoted in ibid., p. 305.

16 Moskowitz, Katz, and Levering, eds., *Everybody's Business* p. 533.

17 William Lyon Mackenzie King, *Industry and Humanity: A Study in the Principles Underlying Industrial Reconstruction* (Toronto: Thomas Allen, 1918), p. 435.

18 Ibid., p. 436.

19 Moskowitz, Katz, and Levering, eds., *Everybody's Business,* p. 534.

20 McGovern and Guttridge, *Coalfield War,* p. 320.

21 Anthony Sampson, *The Seven Sisters: The Great Oil Companies & the World They Shaped* (New York: Viking Press, 1975), p. 38.

22 Quoted in Collier and Horowitz, *The Rockefellers,* p. 122.

23 McGovern and Guttridge, *Coalfield War,* p. 318.

24 Ibid., p. 310.

25 Mackenzie King, *Industry and Humanity,* p. 438.

26 Quoted in Collier and Horowitz, *The Rockefellers,* p. 129.

27 Ibid., p. 129.

28 McGovern and Guttridge, *Coalfield War,* p. 334.

29 Ibid., p. 129.

30 Mackenzie King, *Industry and Humanity,* p. 438.

31 Collier and Horowitz, *The Rockefellers,* p. 113.

32 McGovern and Guttridge, *Coalfield War,* pp. 335-36.

33 Quoted in Collier and Horowitz, *The Rockefellers,* p. 130-31.

34 Ibid., p. 121.

35 Stacey, *Double Life,* p. 226.

36 Moskowitz, Katz, and Levering, eds., *Everybody's Business,* pp. 534-35.

37 Ibid., p. 535.

38 Mackenzie King, *Industry and Humanity,* p. 490.

39 Ibid., pp. 187–88.

40 Stacey, *Double Life*, p. 22.

41 Hardy, *John Grierson*, p. 31.

42 Ibid., p. 33.

43 Eduardo Galeano, *Memory of Fire*, vol. 3: *Century of the Wind* (New York: Pantheon Books, 1988), pp. 120–21.

44 Charles Higham, *Errol Flynn: The Untold Story* (Garden City, N.Y.: Doubleday, 1980), p. 78.

45 Hardy, *John Grierson*, p. 33.

46 Ibid.

47 Ibid., p. 31.

48 Clinton Rossiter and James Lare, eds., *The Essential Lippmann: A Political Philosophy for Liberal Democracy* (Cambridge, Mass.: Harvard University Press, 1982), p. 91.

49 Ibid.

50 Ibid., p. 92.

51 Ibid.

52 The conventional view is that Grierson's subsequent work is evidence that he disagreed with Lippmann's analysis and was determined to use the documentary for "educational" purposes so that the public would be less "bewildered" by modern society and its developments. This view is repeated even by Stuart Hood, who writes that Lippmann, despite his "condescending view of John Citizen ... inspired Grierson with the belief that film could explain the workings of society not in a fictional but a 'documentary' way and thus allow John Citizen (and his wife?) to make better judgements" (Stuart Hood, "John Grierson and the Documentary Film Movement", in *British Cinema History*, James Curran and Vincent Porter, eds. [London: Weidenfeld and Nicolson, 1983], p. 100). This view is part of the mystification surrounding the word "documentary". Interestingly, its practitioners interviewed by Elizabeth Sussex refer often to their "public-relations films", thereby opening up a perspective more rooted in the realities of actual sponsorship and public-relations thinking at the time.

53 Hardy, *John Grierson*, p. 34.

54 Quoted in ibid.

55 Ibid., p. 35.

56 Ibid., p. 36.

57 Ibid., pp. 38–39.

58 Ibid., p. 38.

59 Ibid., p. 45.

60 Ibid., p. 47.
61 Ibid., p. 45.

Chapter Two: The Age of Consent

1 Quoted in Forsyth Hardy, *John Grierson: A Documentary Biography* (London: Faber & Faber, 1979), p. 45.
2 Milton Moskowitz, Michael Katz, and Robert Levering, eds., *Everybody's Business: An Almanac* (San Francisco: Harper & Row, 1980), pp. 499-503.
3 Garth Jowett, "American Domination of the Motion Picture Industry: Canada As a Test Case," in Seth Feldman and Joyce Nelson, eds., *Canadian Film Reader* (Toronto: Peter Martin Associates, 1977), p. 5.
4 Ibid., p. 7
5 Ibid., p. 5.
6 Ibid., p. 7.
7 Hardy, *John Grierson,* p. 47.
8 Ibid., p. 46.
9 Ibid., pp. 47-48.
10 Elizabeth Sussex, *The Rise and Fall of British Documentary: The Story of the Film Movement Founded by John Grierson* (Berkeley: University of California Press, 1975), p. 42.
11 Ibid., pp. 32-33.
12 Quoted in ibid., pp. 14-15.
13 Stuart Hood, "John Grierson and the Documentary Film Movement," in James Curran and Vincent Porter, eds., *British Cinema History* (London: Weidenfeld and Nicolson, 1983), p. 102.
14 Ibid.
15 Forsyth Hardy, ed., *Grierson On Documentary* (London: Faber & Faber, 1946), pp. 48-49.
16 Ibid., p. 39.
17 Charles Higham, *Trading with the Enemy: An Exposé of the Nazi–American Money Plot, 1933-1949* (New York: Delacorte Press, 1983), p. 178.
18 Hardy, ed., *Grierson On Documentary,* pp. 78.
19 Ibid., p. 64.
20 Quoted in Sussex, *Rise and Fall,* p. 33.
21 Quoted in ibid., p. 32.
22 Quoted in ibid.
23 Hood, "John Grierson," p. 103.
24 Erwin Leiser, *Nazi Cinema* (London: Secker & Warburg, 1975), p. 10.
25 Ibid., p. 14.
26 Hardy, ed., *Grierson On Documentary,* p. 77.

27 Sussex, *Rise and Fall,* p. 42.

28 Ibid.

29 Hood, "John Grierson," p. 100.

30 Ibid., p. 107.

31 Quoted in Sussex, *Rise and Fall,* pp. 80-81.

32 Quoted in ibid.

33 Hardy, ed., *Grierson On Documentary,* pp. 112-13.

34 Peter Collier and David Horowitz, *The Rockefellers: An American Dynasty* (New York: Holt, Rinehart and Winston, 1976), p. 152.

35 Hardy, *John Grierson,* p. 89.

36 Ibid., p. 63.

37 Ibid.

38 Quoted in ibid.

39 Ibid.

40 Ibid.

41 Hood, "John Grierson," p. 102.

42 Quoted in ibid., p. 108.

43 Quoted in Sussex, *Rise and Fall,* p. 82.

44 Quoted in ibid., p. 60.

45 See Hardy, *John Grierson,* pp. 83-84; and Sussex, *Rise and Fall,* p. 61.

46 Anthony Sampson, *The Seven Sisters: The Great Oil Companies & The World They Shaped* (New York: Viking Press, 1975), p. 63. The company went through a number of name changes, growing rapidly first as Anglo-Persian, then as Anglo-Iranian, and then as British Petroleum.

47 Ibid., p. 82.

48 Ibid., p. 83.

49 Ibid., p. 68.

50 Eduardo Galeano, *Memory of Fire,* vol. 3: *Century of the Wind* (New York: Pantheon Books, 1988), pp. 98-99.

51 Sampson, *Seven Sisters,* p. 86.

52 Ibid., p. 87.

53 Galeano, *Memory of Fire,* vol. 3, p. 82.

54 Ibid., p. 94.

55 Higham, *Trading with the Enemy,* p. 33.

56 Sampson, *Seven Sisters,* p. 91.

57 Higham, *Trading with the Enemy,* p. 33.

58 See, for example, William L. Shirer, *The Rise and Fall of the Third Reich: A History of Nazi Germany* (New York: Fawcett Crest, 1962); and Klaus Hildebrand, *The Third Reich* (London: George Allen & Unwin, 1984).

59 Sampson, *Seven Sisters,* p. 96.

60 Ibid.
61 Quoted in Sussex, *Rise and Fall,* pp. 60-61.
62 Hood, "John Grierson," p. 104.
63 Sampson, *Seven Sisters,* pp. 68-69.
64 Trevor Ryan, "'The New Road to Progress': The Use and Production of Films by the Labour Movement, 1929-39," in Curran and Porter, eds., *British Cinema History,* p. 123. There are several occasions in Sussex's *Rise and Fall* when her interviewees refer to themselves as having been "snobs" during the 1930s and proud of their Cambridge backgrounds. Grierson told Sussex that in the documentary movement "the intellectual vanity, the academic vanity, was total from the beginning", suggesting the class bias prevalent in the films (p. 21).
65 Sussex, *Rise and Fall,* p. 80.
66 Hardy, ed., *Grierson On Documentary,* p. 68.
67 Yvette Hackett, "The National Film Society of Canada, 1935-1951: Its Origins and Development," in Gene Walz, ed., *Flashback: People and Institutions in Canadian Film History* (Montreal: Mediatext Publications, 1986), p. 141.
68 Gary Evans, *John Grierson and the National Film Board: The Politics of Wartime Propaganda* (Toronto: University of Toronto Press, 1984), p. 52.
69 Ibid., p. 49.
70 Quoted in ibid., p. 48.
71 Ibid.
72 Ibid.
73 Sussex, *Rise and Fall,* p. 93.
74 Telephone interview with Gary Evans by the author, autumn 1986.
75 Evans, *Grierson and the* NFB, p. 49.
76 Ibid., p. 53.
77 Hardy, *John Grierson,* p. 90.
78 C.P. Stacey, *A Very Double Life* (Halifax: Formac / Goodread Biographies, 1976), p. 119.
79 William Lyon Mackenzie King, *Industry and Humanity: A Study in the Principles Underlying Industrial Reconstruction* (Toronto: Thomas Allen, 1918), p. 223.
80 Hardy, *John Grierson,* p. 114.

Chapter Three: Spectacle, Absences, and the Economy of God

1 Forsyth Hardy, *John Grierson: A Documentary Biography* (London: Faber & Faber, 1979), p. 93.
2 Quoted in ibid.

3 John Herd Thompson, with Allen Seager, *Canada, 1922-1939: Decades of Discord* (Toronto: McClelland and Stewart, 1986), p. 227.
4 Ibid., p. 226. Many of those early 1930s deportees were returned to countries where their lives would be endangered by the developing political climate.
5 Quoted in ibid., pp. 226–27.
6 Ibid., p. 223.
7 Hardy, *John Grierson,* p. 95.
8 Ibid.
9 Ibid.
10 Ibid., p. 96.
11 Quoted in Robert M. Stamp, *The World of Tomorrow: A View of Canada in 1939* (Toronto: Fitzhenry & Whiteside, 1985), pp. 26–28.
12 Quoted in Hardy, *John Grierson,* p. 100.
13 Stamp, *World of Tomorrow,* pp. 80–88.
14 Quoted in ibid., p. 87.
15 Dallas W. Smythe, *Dependency Road: Communications, Capitalism, Consciousness, and Canada* (Norwood, N.J.: Ablex, 1981), p. 100.
16 Stamp, *World of Tomorrow,* p. 87.
17 Ibid., p. 84.
18 Ibid., p. 93.
19 Ibid.
20 Quoted in ibid., p. 94. Emphasis mine.
21 Quoted in ibid.
22 William Lyon Mackenzie King, *Industry and Humanity: A Study in the Principles Underlying Industrial Reconstruction* (Toronto: Thomas Allen, 1918), p. 34.
23 Ibid., p. 49.
24 Ibid.
25 Ibid.
26 Ibid., p. 50.
27 Ibid.
28 Ibid., p. 363.
29 J.L. Granatstein, Irving M. Abella, David J. Bercuson, R. Craig Brown, H. Blair Neatby, *Twentieth Century Canada* (Toronto: McGraw-Hill Ryerson, 1983), p. 196.
30 Thompson, *Canada, 1922-1939,* p. 195.
31 Ibid., p. 279.
32 Ibid., p. 331.
33 Quoted in C.P. Stacey, *Canada and the Age of Conflict,* vol. 2: *1921-1948, The Mackenzie King Era* (Toronto: University of Toronto Press, 1981), p. 195.

34 Tony Wilden, *The Imaginary Canadian: An Examination for Discovery* (Vancouver: Pulp Press, 1980), p. 51.
35 Ibid., p. 3.
36 Northrop Frye, *The Bush Garden: Essays on the Canadian Imagination* (Toronto: House of Anansi Press, 1971), p. 1.
37 Frantz Fanon, *The Wretched of the Earth* (New York: Grove Press, 1968), p. 250.
38 Frye, *Bush Garden,* p. 220.
39 Smythe, *Dependency Road,* p. x.
40 Ibid.
41 Quoted in ibid., p. 95.
42 Quoted in ibid.
43 Thompson, *Canada, 1922-1939,* p. 332.
44 See especially William L. Shirer, *Rise and Fall of the Third Reich: A History of Nazi Germany* (New York: Fawcett Crest, 1962).
45 James H. Gray, *The Winter Years: The Depression on the Prairies* (Toronto: Macmillan, 1966), pp. 126-27.
46 Ibid., p. 132.
47 Thompson, *Canada, 1922-1939,* p. 322.
48 Bruce Kidd, "Canadian Opposition to the 1936 Olympics in Germany," *Canadian Journal of the History of Sport and Physical Education* 9, no. 2 (1978): 20-40. Also cited in Thompson, *Canada, 1922-1939,* p. 322.
49 Thompson, *Canada, 1922-1939,* p.317.
50 Ibid., p. 318.
51 Stacey, *Canada and the Age of Conflict,* vol. 2, p. 210.
52 Charles Higham, *Trading with the Enemy: An Exposé of the Nazi–American Money Plot, 1933-1949* (New York: Delacorte Press, 1983), p. 6.
53 Quoted in Stacey, *Canada and the Age of Conflict,* vol. 2, p. 213.
54 Quoted in ibid., p. 248.
55 Quoted in ibid., p. 249.
56 Bertram Gross, *Friendly Fascism: The New Face of Power in America* (Montreal: Black Rose Books, 1980), p. 19.
57 Marjorie McKay, "History of the National Film Board," unpublished and undated manuscript, NFB Archives, Montreal, p. 49.
58 Gary Evans, *John Grierson and the National Film Board: The Politics of Wartime Propaganda* (Toronto: University of Toronto Press, 1984), p. 53.
59 Forsyth Hardy, ed., *Grierson On Documentary* (London: Faber & Faber, 1946), p. 207.
60 Peter Morris, ed., NFB: *The War Years* (Ottawa: Canadian Film Institute, 1965), p. 1.

Chapter Four: The Curse of Nations

1 Forsyth Hardy, *John Grierson: A Documentary Biography* (London: Faber & Faber, 1979), p. 100
2 Quoted in ibid.
3 Ibid., p. 101.
4 Quoted in Marjorie McKay, "History of the National Film Board," unpublished and undated manuscript, NFB Archives, Montreal, p. 9.
5 Quoted in ibid.
6 Gary Evans, *John Grierson and the National Film Board: The Politics of Wartime Propaganda* (Toronto: University of Toronto Press, 1984), p. 63.
7 Hardy, *John Grierson,* p. 101.
8 Evans, *John Grierson and the* NFB, pp. 52-53.
9 Hardy, *John Grierson,* pp. 94, 110.
10 Quoted in ibid., p. 94.
11 Evans, *John Grierson and the* NFB, p. 77.
12 Quoted in Hardy, *John Grierson,* p. 110.
13 Elizabeth Sussex, *The Rise and Fall of British Documentary: The Story of the Film Movement Founded by John Grierson* (Berkeley: University of California Press, 1975), p. 121.
14 Ibid.
15 Quoted in ibid., p. 92.
16 Hardy, *John Grierson,* p. 112.
17 Quoted in Evans, *John Grierson and the* NFB, p. 78.
18 Ibid., p. 78.
19 Ibid., p. 81.
20 Ibid.
21 Ibid., p. 82.
22 Ernst Borneman, "Documentary Films: World War II," in Seth Feldman and Joyce Nelson, eds., *Canadian Film Reader* (Toronto: Peter Martin Associates, 1977), p. 51.
23 Quoted in Jack Ellis, "Grierson's First Years at the NFB," in Feldman and Nelson, eds., *Canadian Film Reader,* p. 41.
24 Forsyth Hardy, ed., *Grierson On Documentary* (London: Faber & Faber, 1946), p. 206.
25 Quoted in McKay, "History of the NFB," p. 28.
26 Evans, *John Grierson and the* NFB, pp. 32-33.
27 Quoted in Hardy, *John Grierson,* p. 127; from a letter written in June 1942.
28 Hardy, ed., *Grierson On Documentary,* p. 106.
29 Ibid., p. 144.

30 Hardy, *John Grierson,* p. 110.
31 Ibid., p. 120.
32 Evans, *John Grierson and the* NFB, p. 113.
33 David Clandfield, *Canadian Film* (Toronto: Oxford University Press, 1987), p. 18.
34 Peter Morris, ed., NFB*: The War Years* (Ottawa: Canadian Film Institute, 1965), p. 27.
35 Ibid.
36 Evans, *John Grierson and the* NFB, p. 169.
37 Ibid., pp. 296–300.
38 Ibid., p. 119.
39 Hardy, *John Grierson,* p. 120.
40 Donald W. Buchanan, "The Projection of Canada," in Morris, ed., NFB*: The War Years,* p. 16.
41 Hardy, *John Grierson,* p. 120.
42 McKay, "History of the NFB," p. 27.
43 Evans, *John Grierson and the* NFB, p. 120.
44 Ibid., pp. 116–17.
45 Hardy, *John Grierson,* p. 205.
46 Hardy, ed., *Grierson On Documentary,* p. 106.
47 Evans, *John Grierson and the* NFB, p. 32.
48 Hardy, *John Grierson,* p. 58.
49 Evans, *John Grierson and the* NFB, p. 32.
50 Ibid., pp. 32–33.
51 Borneman, "Documentary Films," p. 55.
52 Hardy, ed., *Grierson On Documentary,* p. 111.
53 Jack Ellis, "John Grierson's Relation with British Documentary During World War Two," in The John Grierson Project–McGill University, eds., *John Grierson and the* NFB (Toronto: ECW Press, 1984), p. 63.
54 *Canada in World War II: Post-War Possibilities* (Montreal: William S. Boas, 1945), p. 7.
55 Ibid., p. 72.
56 C.P. Stacey, *Canada and the Age of Conflict,* vol. 2: *1921-1948, The Mackenzie King Era* (Toronto: University of Toronto Press, 1981), p. 359.
57 Ibid.
58 Borneman, "Documentary Films," p. 53.
59 Hardy, ed., *Grierson On Documentary,* p. 205.
60 McKay, "History of the NFB," p. 49.
61 Ibid., p. 45.

62 Evans, *John Grierson and the* NFB, p. 256.
63 John Grierson, "A Film Policy for Canada," *Canadian Affairs,* June 14, 1944, p. 6.
64 Quoted in Hardy, *John Grierson,* p. 114.
65 McKay, "History of the NFB," p. 18.
66 Borneman, "Documentary Films," pp. 50, 53.
67 Margaret Atwood, *Survival: A Thematic Guide to Canadian Literature* (Toronto: House of Anansi Press, 1972), p. 17.
68 Peter Harcourt, "The Innocent Eye," in Feldman and Nelson, eds., *Canadian Film Reader,* p. 72.
69 Ibid.
70 Hardy, ed., *Grierson On Documentary,* p. 106.
71 "The Grierson Workshop," *Pot Pourri,* Summer, 1975, p. 9.
72 Hardy, ed., *Grierson On Documentary,* p. 126.
73 Harcourt, "Innocent Eye," p. 73.
74 D.B. Jones, *Movies and Memoranda: An Interpretive History of the National Film Board of Canada* (Ottawa: Canadian Film Institute, 1981), p. 90.
75 Harcourt, "Innocent Eye," p. 73.
76 Peter Morris, *Embattled Shadows: A History of Canadian Cinema 1895-1939* (Montreal: McGill-Queen's University Press, 1978), p. 241.
77 See Peter Morris, "After Grierson: The National Film Board, 1945-1953," in Seth Feldman, ed., *Take One* (Toronto: Irwin Publishing, 1984), p. 185; and Thomas Waugh, "Action Stations: Joris Ivens and the National Film Board," in Gene Walz, ed., *Flashback: People and Institutions in Canadian Film History* (Montreal: Mediatext Publications, 1986), p. 51.
78 McKay, "History of the NFB," p. 49.
79 Ibid.
80 Ibid.
81 Barbara Halpern Martineau, "Before the Guerillieres: Women's Films at the NFB During World War II," in Feldman and Nelson, eds., *Canadian Film Reader,* p. 64.
82 Ibid.
83 Ruth Roach Pierson, *Canadian Women and the Second World War* (Ottawa: Canadian Historical Association, 1983), p. 19.
84 Sussex, *Rise and Fall,* p. 86.
85 Evans, *John Grierson and the* NFB, p. 145.
86 Ibid., p. 223.
87 Tony Wilden, *The Imaginary Canadian: An Examination for Discovery* (Vancouver: Pulp Press, 1981), p. 52.

88 Northrop Frye, *The Bush Garden: Essays on the Canadian Imagination* (Toronto: House of Anansi Press, 1971), p. 219.

89 Anthony Sampson, *The Seven Sisters: The Great Oil Companies & the World They Shaped* (New York: Viking Press, 1975), pp. 101–102.

90 Hardy, ed., *Grierson On Documentary*, p. 128.

Chapter Five: Grierson and Hollywood's Canada

1 Quoted in Erwin Leiser, *Nazi Cinema* (London: Secker & Warburg, 1975), p. 61.

2 Quoted in ibid., p. 47.

3 Quoted in ibid., p. 60.

4 John Grierson, "A Film Policy for Canada," *Canadian Affairs,* June 14, 1944, p. 12.

5 Quoted in "The Grierson Workshop," *Pot Pourri,* Summer 1975, p. 12.

6 Quoted in John Herd Thompson, with Allen Seager, *Canada, 1922-1939: Decades of Discord* (Toronto: McClelland and Stewart, 1986), p. 177.

7 Ibid.

8 Manjunath Pendakur, "Canadian Dreams and American Control: Political Economy of the Canadian Film Industry," an early draft of a book manuscript to be published by Wayne State University Press, p. 78. My thanks to Manjunath Pendakur, associate professor at Northwestern University, for permission to quote from this draft.

9 Ibid., p. 79.

10 Peter Morris, *Embattled Shadows: A History of Canadian Cinema 1895-1939* (Montreal: McGill-Queen's University Press, 1978), p. 179.

11 Pendakur, "Canadian Dreams," p. 80.

12 Michael Spencer, "US–Canada Film Relations 1920-1986," *Cinema Canada,* June, 1986, p. 12.

13 Pendakur, "Canadian Dreams," p. 80.

14 Gary Evans, *John Grierson and the National Film Board: The Politics of Wartime Propaganda* (Toronto: University of Toronto Press, 1984), p. 55.

15 Forsyth Hardy, ed., *Grierson On Documentary* (London: Faber & Faber, 1946), p. 87.

16 "Movie Quiz," *Canadian Affairs,* June 15, 1944, back cover. The quiz question reads: "How much do Canadians spend in a year on admission to the movies?" The answer: "$58 million in 1942." Another question asks: "How often do you think the average Canadian went to the movies, say in 1942?" The answer: "3½ million Canadians go each week" (i.e., 182 million admissions in 1942).

17 Forsyth Hardy, *John Grierson: A Documentary Biography* (London: Faber & Faber, 1979), p. 102.
18 Gary Evans, *John Grierson and the National Film Board: The Politics of Wartime Propaganda* (Toronto: University of Toronto Press, 1984), p. 73.
19 Ibid., p. 164. According to Elizabeth Sussex (*The Rise and Fall of British Documentary: The Story of the Film Movement Founded by John Grierson* [Berkeley: University of California Press, 1975], p. 87), Grierson in 1937 became a consultant to de Rochemont's *March of Time* London office.
20 Evans, *John Grierson and the* NFB, p. 166.
21 Peter Morris, "Backwards to the Future: John Grierson's Film Policy for Canada," in Gene Walz, ed., *Flashback: People and Institutions in Canadian Film History* (Montreal: Mediatext Publications, 1986), pp. 17-35.
22 Ibid., p. 24.
23 Pendakur, "Canadian Dreams," p. 92.
24 Hardy, *John Grierson,* p. 111.
25 Quoted in Morris, "Backwards to the Future," p. 25.
26 Hardy, *John Grierson,* p. 121.
27 Susan Sontag, *Under the Sign of Saturn* (New York: Vintage Books, 1981), pp. 80-81.
28 Ibid., p. 81.
29 Ibid., p. 80.
30 Hardy, *John Grierson,* p. 261.
31 Richard Schickel, *The Disney Version: The Life, Times, Art and Commerce of Walt Disney* (New York: Simon and Shuster, 1968), p. 251.
32 Ibid.
33 Ibid.
34 Hardy, *John Grierson,* pp. 150, 159.
35 Grierson, "Film Policy," pp. 9-10.
36 Morris, "Backwards to the Future," p. 18.
37 Pierre Berton, *Hollywood's Canada: The Americanization of Our National Image* (Toronto: McClelland and Stewart, 1975), p. 172.
38 Morris, "Backwards to the Future," p. 31.
39 Ibid., p. 23.
40 Sussex, *Rise and Fall,* p. 120.
41 Margaret Dickinson, "The State and the Consolidation of Monopoly," in James Curran and Vincent Porter, eds., *British Cinema History* (London: Weidenfeld and Nicolson, 1983), p. 79.
42 Quoted in ibid.
43 Ibid., p. 82.

44 Ibid., pp. 82–83. Emphasis mine.
45 See Kirwan Cox, "The Grierson Files," *Cinema Canada,* June / July 1979, pp. 16–18.
46 Ibid., p. 18.
47 U.S. Department of State, "Freedom of the Press—World-wide," Bulletin no. 14, February 3, 1946, p. 160. Cited in Pendakur, "Canadian Dreams," p. 12.
48 Peter Collier and David Horowitz, *The Rockefellers: An American Dynasty* (New York: Holt, Rinehart and Winston, 1976), pp. 228.
49 Ibid., p. 232.
50 Charles Higham, *Trading with the Enemy: An Exposé of the Nazi–American Money Plot, 1933-1949* (New York: Delacorte Press, 1983), p. 39.
51 Collier and Horowitz, *The Rockefellers,* p. 262.
52 Schickel, *Disney Version,* p. 263.
53 Ibid. For an interesting analysis of Disney's propagandist effort in Latin America, see Ariel Dorfman and Armand Mattelart, *How to Read Donald Duck: Imperialist Ideology in the Disney Comic* (New York: International General, 1975).
54 Collier and Horowitz, *The Rockefellers,* p. 236.
55 Quoted in ibid.
56 Quoted in ibid.
57 Ibid.
58 Quoted in Stuart Hood, "John Grierson and the Documentary Film Movement," in Curran and Porter, eds., *British Cinema History,* p. 104.
59 Ibid.
60 Evans, *John Grierson and the* NFB, p. 38.
61 Quoted in Morris, "Backwards to the Future," p. 22. Emphasis mine.

Chapter Six: Designs for Living and Dying

1 C.P. Stacey, *Canada and the Age of Conflict,* vol. 2: *1921-1948, The Mackenzie King Era* (Toronto: University of Toronto Press, 1981), p. 327.
2 Ibid.
3 J.L. Granatstein, *The Ottawa Men: The Civil Service Mandarins, 1935-1957* (Toronto: Oxford University Press, 1982), p. 93.
4 Ibid., p. 92.
5 Gary Evans, *John Grierson and the National Film Board: The Politics of Wartime Propaganda* (Toronto: University of Toronto Press, 1984), p. 236.
6 Robert Harris and Jeremy Paxman, *A Higher Form of Killing: The Secret Story of Gas and Germ Warfare* (London: Triad / Granada, 1983), p. 176. See also

Barry Broadfoot, *Six War Years: 1939-1945* (Don Mills: Paperjacks, 1974), p. 4. A deserter from the Canadian army at the time states that the chemical warfare tests used "good Canadian soldiers" as the guinea pigs.

7 Harris and Paxman, *A Higher Form of Killing*, p. 177.

8 Peter Pringle and James Spigelman, *The Nuclear Barons* (London: Sphere Books, 1982), pp. 140-43.

9 Forsyth Hardy, ed., *Grierson On Documentary* (London: Faber & Faber, 1946), pp. 111-12.

10 Ibid., p. 130.

11 Quoted in Forsyth Hardy, *John Grierson: A Documentary Biography* (London: Faber & Faber, 1979), p. 126.

12 Hardy, ed., *Grierson On Documentary*, pp. 135-36.

13 Frantz Fanon, *The Wretched of the Earth* (New York: Grove Press, 1968), p. 189.

14 Quoted in Anthony Sampson, *The Seven Sisters: The Great Oil Companies & the World They Shaped* (New York: Viking Press, 1975), p. 30.

15 Hardy, ed., *Grierson On Documentary*, p. 134.

16 Ibid., pp. 108-109. Emphasis mine.

17 Ibid., p 117.

18 Ibid., pp. 138-39.

19 Ibid., p. 117.

20 Ibid., p. 139. Emphasis mine.

21 Ibid., p. 117.

22 Ibid., p. 137.

23 Evans, *John Grierson and the* NFB, p. 116.

24 Ibid.

25 Ibid., p. 181.

26 Irving Abella and Harold Troper, *None Is Too Many: Canada and the Jews of Europe, 1933-1948* (Toronto: Lester & Orpen Dennys, 1983).

27 J.L. Granatstein and J.M. Hitsman, *Broken Promises: A History of Conscription in Canada* (Toronto: Copp Clark Pitman, 1985), p. 123.

28 James H. Gray, *The Winter Years: The Depression on the Prairies* (Toronto: Macmillan, 1966), p. 143.

29 Ibid., 148.

30 Eric Koch, *Deemed Suspect* (Toronto: Methuen, 1980).

31 Ann Gomer Sunahara, *The Politics of Racism: The Uprooting of Japanese Canadians During the Second World War* (Toronto: James Lorimer, 1981), p. 4.

32 Hardy, ed., *Grierson On Documentary*, pp. 131-32.

33 Ibid., p. 117.

34 Ibid., p. 126.

35 Ibid., p. 122.

36 Margaret Ann Elton, "The Images of Canada: An Appraisal of the Eye, the Mind, and the Teaching of John Grierson," in The John Grierson Project–McGill University, eds., *John Grierson and the* NFB (Toronto: ECW Press, 1984), p. 81.

37 Ruth Roach Pierson, *'They're Still Women After All': The Second World War And Canadian Womanhood* (Toronto: McClelland and Stewart, 1986), p. 72.

38 Hardy, ed., *Grierson On Documentary*, p. 153.

39 Jack Ellis, "John Grierson's Relation with British Documentary During World War Two," in The John Grierson Project–McGill University, eds., *John Grierson and the* NFB (Toronto: ECW Press, 1984), p. 63.

40 Hardy, ed., *Grierson On Documentary*, p. 129.

Chapter Seven: The Pursuit of Sacrifice

1 Siegfried Giedion, *Mechanization Takes Command: A Contribution to Anonymous History* (New York: W.W. Norton, 1948), p. 121.

2 Jeffrey Herf, *Reactionary Modernism: Technology, Culture and Politics in Weimar and the Third Reich* (Cambridge: Cambridge University Press, 1984).

3 See, for example, Adolf Hitler, *Mein Kampf,* Ralph Manheim, trans. (Boston: Houghton Mifflin, 1943), p. 639.

4 Charles Higham, *Trading with the Enemy: An Exposé of the Nazi–American Money Plot, 1933-1949* (New York: Delacorte Press, 1983), p. 178.

5 Quoted in Herf, *Reactionary Modernism,* p. 196.

6 One need only consider the reaction of U.S. scientists to the first test of the atomic bomb (code-named "Trinity") to detect a similar projection of emotion and soul into technology. Various accounts of the Trinity test reveal that many of the scientists present experienced spontaneous spiritual reactions to the mushroom-cloud. In his book *Day One: Before Hiroshima and After* (New York: Warner Books, 1985, p. 231), Peter Wyden indicates that the scientists present at Trinity erupted in "swirling euphoria ... like primitive man dancing at one of his fire festivals at the coming of spring". The subsequent decision to use the bomb on Japan, a nation already defeated through the means of conventional warfare, was not entirely based on reason as the motivating factor.

7 Peter Morris, "Re-Thinking Grierson: The Ideology Of John Grierson," speech delivered to the FSAC / AQEC Conference, Montreal, 1986, pp. 33-34.

8 Bertram Gross, *Friendly Fascism: The New Face of Power in America* (Montreal: Black Rose Books, 1980). p. 27.

9 Ibid.

10 Ibid. See also Robert Jungk, *Brighter Than a Thousand Suns: A Personal*

History of the Atomic Scientists (Harmondsworth: Penguin, 1960) for an analysis of the weakness of the German scientific technostructure.

11 Forsyth Hardy, *John Grierson: A Documentary Biography* (London: Faber & Faber, 1979), p. 105.
12 Forsyth Hardy, ed., *Grierson On Documentary* (London: Faber & Faber, 1946), pp. 136–37.
13 Ibid., p. 128.
14 Margaret Ann Elton, "The Images of Canada: An Appraisal of the Eye, the Mind, and the Teaching of John Grierson," in The John Grierson Project–McGill University, eds., *John Grierson and the* NFB (Toronto: ECW Press, 1984), p. 81.
15 Evans, *John Grierson and the* NFB, p. 157.
16 Morris, "Re-Thinking Grierson," p. 29.
17 Quoted in J.P. Stern, *Hitler: The Fuhrer and the People* (London: Flamingo Press, 1984), p. 33
18 Morris, "Re-Thinking Grierson," pp. 29–30.
19 Hardy, ed., *Grierson On Documentary,* p. 121.
20 Ibid., p. 126.
21 Ibid., p. 143.
22 Ibid., pp. 175–76.
23 Ibid., p. 127.
24 Hardy, *John Grierson,* p. 144.
25 Hardy, ed., *Grierson On Documentary,* p. 177.
26 Gross, *Friendly Fascism,* p. 28. I am, however, indebted to Peter Morris' speech "Re-Thinking Grierson" for the initial indication of this political meaning.
27 Hardy, ed., *Grierson On Documentary,* p. 118.
28 Higham, in *Trading with the Enemy* (p. xvi) notes that "the bosses of the multinationals as we know them today had a six-spot on every side of the dice cube. Whichever side won the war, the powers that really ran nations would not be adversely affected."
29 Ibid., p. xiv.
30 Ibid., p. xv.
31 Peter Collier and David Horowitz, *The Rockefellers: An American Dynasty* (New York: Holt, Rinehart and Winston, 1976), pp. 225.
32 Tom Bower, *Blind Eye To Murder: Britain, America and the Purging of Nazi Germany—A Pledge Betrayed* (London: Andre Deutsch, 1981), p. 18.
33 Collier and Horowitz, *The Rockefellers,* p. 225.
34 Quoted in Higham, *Trading with the Enemy,* p. 57.
35 Gross, *Friendly Fascism,* p. 20.

36 Higham, *Trading with the Enemy*, p. xvi.

37 Robert Bothwell and William Kilbourn, *C.D. Howe: A Biography* (Toronto: McClelland and Stewart, 1979), pp. 169-70. See also C.P. Stacey, *Canada and the Age of Conflict*, vol. 2: *1921-1948, The Mackenzie King Era* (Toronto: University of Toronto Press, 1981), p. 331.

38 Hardy, *John Grierson*, p. 152.

39 Hardy, ed., *Grierson On Documentary*, p. 116.

40 William Lyon Mackenzie King, *Industry and Humanity: A Study in the Principles Underlying Industrial Reconstruction* (Toronto: Thomas Allen, 1918), p. 17; the complete passage is as follows: "The time may come when communities as a whole will be so sensitive to social views that it may be possible to differentiate their conflicting elements as accurately as in the human body, scientists differentiate blood corpuscles from pathological germs. By a minute regard for actions and tendencies, it may become possible to brand those individuals who are life-destroying germs in human society. When that time comes, the corpuscles of the body politic may combine as effectively to destroy its pathological germs, as, in the human body, white corpuscles combine, and seek to destroy the germs of disease."

Chapter Eight: The Anxious Mosaic

1 Quoted in C.P. Stacey, *Canada and the Age of Conflict*, vol. 2: *1921-1948, The Mackenzie King Era* (Toronto: University of Toronto Press, 1981), p. 211.

2 Eric Koch, *Deemed Suspect* (Toronto: Methuen, 1980), p. xiv.

3 Ibid., p. 188. Grierson obviously knew about these internments; he arranged to have one of the inmates, Ernst Borneman, released to work at the NFB.

4 Quoted in William and Kathleen Repka, *Dangerous Patriots: Canada's Unknown Prisoners of War* (Vancouver: New Star Books, 1982), p. 14.

5 Ibid.

6 Koch, *Deemed Suspect*, p. 163.

7 Ibid., p. 26.

8 John Melady, *Escape From Canada* (Toronto: Macmillan, 1981).

9 Barry Broadfoot, *Six War Years: 1939-1945* (Don Mills: Paperjacks, 1974), pp. 533-34.

10 Ann Gomer Sunahara, *The Politics of Racism: The Uprooting of Japanese Canadians During the Second World War* (Toronto: James Lorimer, 1981), pp. 77-78.

11 Ibid., p. 78.

12 Broadfoot, *Six War Years*, p. 109.

13 Quoted in D.B. Jones, *Movies and Memoranda* (Ottawa: Canadian Film Institute, 1981), p. 30. Emphasis mine.

14 See especially Ian Lockerbie, "Grierson and Realism," in The John Grierson Project–McGill University, eds., *John Grierson and the* NFB (Toronto: ECW Press, 1984), p. 87.
15 Donald Buchanan, "Canadian Movies Promote Citizenship," undated photocopy of article, publication unknown; housed in the NFB Print Archives, Montreal, p. 120.
16 Gary Evans, *John Grierson and the National Film Board: The Politics of Wartime Propaganda* (Toronto: University of Toronto Press, 1984), p. 148.
17 Buchanan, "Canadian Movies," p. 120.
18 Donald Buchanan, "The Projection of Canada," reprinted in Peter Morris, ed., NFB*: The War Years* (Ottawa: Canadian Film Institute, 1965), p. 16.
19 Letter from Donald Cameron, NFB regional agent, November 27, 1942; document housed in the NFB Print Archives, Montreal.
20 Buchanan, "Projection of Canada," p. 9.
21 C.W. Gray, *Movies for the People: The Story of the National Film Board's Unique Distribution System* (Montreal: National Film Board, 1973), p. 42.
22 Evans, *John Grierson and the* NFB, pp. 159-60.
23 Ibid., p. 161.
24 C.W. Gray interview with C. Marshall, wartime projectionist in British Columbia; tape housed in the NFB Print Archives, Montreal.
25 Buchanan, "Canadian Movies," p. 121.
26 Marjorie McKay, "History of the National Film Board," unpublished and undated manuscript, NFB Archives, Montreal, p. 55.
27 Gray, *Movies for the People,* p. 43.
28 Donald Cameron, "Films on Canada's War Effort," information circular, dated January 10, 1942; document housed in the NFB Print Archives, Montreal.
29 Lockerbie, "Grierson and Realism," p. 99.
30 Evans, *John Grierson and the* NFB, pp. 42-43.
31 Gray, *Movies for the People,* p. 44.
32 C.W. Gray, "Circuit Diary: 1942-1945"; document housed in the NFB Print Archives, Montreal, unpaged.
33 Evans, *John Grierson and the* NFB, p. 151.
34 C.W. Gray interview with E.A. Fraser; tape housed in the NFB Print Archives, Montreal.
35 "The Grierson Workshop," *Pot Pourri,* Summer 1975, p. 9.
36 Ibid.
37 Lockerbie, "Grierson and Realism," p. 87.
38 C.W. Gray, early draft for *Movies for the People*; document housed in the NFB Print Archives, Montreal.

39 C.W. Gray interview with Jacques St-Marie, wartime projectionist for Quebec; tape housed in the NFB Print Archives, Montreal.

40 C.W. Gray interview with Vaughn Deacon, NFB regional agent for Ontario; tape housed in the NFB Print Archives, Montreal.

41 Peter Morris, "Backwards to the Future: John Grierson's Film Policy for Canada," in Gene Walz, ed., *Flashback: People and Institutions in Canadian Film History* (Montreal: Mediatext Publications, 1986), p. 27.

42 Ibid., p. 30.

43 Ibid.

44 Quoted in Broadfoot, *Six War Years,* p. 167.

45 "The Grierson Workshop," p. 9.

46 Gray, "Circuit Diary," 1943.

47 Desmond Morton with Terry Copp, *Working People* (Toronto: Deneau Publishers, 1984), p. 153.

48 Quoted in ibid., p. 150.

49 Ibid.

50 Charles Higham, *Trading with the Enemy: An Exposé of the Nazi–American Money Plot, 1933-1949* (New York: Delacorte Press, 1983), pp. 165-66.

51 Ibid. A less virulent form of labour intimidation in Canada was to be found in the Leadership League, a neo-fascist organization spear-headed by George McCullagh, publisher of the *Globe and Mail*. One of the elements of the organization was a paramilitary group known as the Frontiersmen. "These were people who dressed almost the same as the mounted police—the broad, flat-brimmed hat, the breeches, the high boots—though they wore a blue serge jacket with silver epaulets. They were supposed to be a semi-civil-defence outfit but they appeared in those areas where labour organization was taking place." Quoted in Goria Montero, *We Stood Together: First-hand Accounts of Dramatic Events in Canada's Labour Past* (Toronto: James Lorimer, 1979), p. 77.

52 Higham, *Trading with the Enemy,* p. 166.

53 Morton, *Working People,* p. 171.

54 Irving Abella, "Oshawa 1937," in Irving Abella, ed., *On Strike: Six Key Labour Struggles in Canada 1919-1949* (Toronto: James Lorimer, 1975), p. 121.

55 Morton, *Working People,* p. 154.

56 Quoted in Montero, *We Stood Together,* p. 93.

57 Morton, *Working People,* p. 170.

58 Ibid., pp. 170-71.

59 Quoted in Montero, *We Stood Together,* p. 74.

60 Morton, *Working People,* p. 171.

61 Quoted in Repka, *Dangerous Patriots,* p. 150.

62 Quoted in Rick Salutin, *The Organizer: A Canadian Union Life* (Toronto: James Lorimer, 1980), p. 26.
63 David Moulton, "Ford Windsor 1945," in Abella, ed., *On Strike,* p. 130.
64 Peter Pringle and James Spigelman, *The Nuclear Barons* (London: Sphere Books, 1982), p. 141.
65 *Canada in World War II: Post-War Possibilities* (Montreal: William S. Boas, 1945), p. 31.
66 Ibid.
67 Forsyth Hardy, ed., *Grierson On Documentary* (London: Faber & Faber, 1946), pp. 136-37.
68 Robert Bothwell and William Kilbourn, *C.D. Howe: A Biography* (Toronto: McClelland and Stewart, 1980). p. 154.
69 Dallas W. Smythe, *Dependency Road: Communications, Capitalism, Consciousness, and Canada* (Norwood, N.J.: Ablex, 1981), p. 101.
70 Pringle and Spigelman, *Nuclear Barons,* pp. 140-43.
71 Ibid., p. 142.
72 Morton, *Working People,* p. 171.
73 Ibid.
74 Ibid.
75 Quoted in Montero, *We Stood Together,* p. 95.
76 Moulton, "Ford Windsor 1945," p. 131.
77 Ibid., p. 132.
78 Quoted in Bothwell and Kilbourn, *C.D. Howe,* p. 162.
79 Evans, *John Grierson and the* NFB, p. 103.
80 Morton, *Working People,* pp. 182-83.
81 Quoted in Montero, *We Stood Together,* pp. 118-19.
82 Morton, *Working People,* pp. 182-83.
83 Ibid.
84 Evans, *John Grierson and the* NFB, p. 102.
85 Quoted in ibid.
86 Morton, *Working People,* p. 183.
87 Evans, *John Grierson and the* NFB, p. 102.
88 Ibid., p. 103.
89 Gray, *Movies for the People,* p. 50.
90 Ibid.
91 "Minutes of Meeting," National Trade Union Film Committee, April 17, 1945; document housed in the NFB Print Archives, Montreal.
92 Gray interview with Deacon.
93 Evans, *John Grierson and the* NFB, p. 153.
94 Gray interview with Deacon.
95 Gray, *Movies for the People,* p. 52.

96 William Lyon Mackenzie King, *Industry and Humanity: A Study in the Principles Underlying Industrial Reconstruction* (Toronto: Thomas Allen, 1918), p. 466.
97 Ibid.
98 Ibid.
99 Quoted in ibid., p. 452.
100 Gray, *Movies for the People*, pp. 50, 52.
101 Hardy, ed., *Grierson On Documentary*, p. 127.
102 Gray, *Movies for the People*, p. 43.
103 Ibid., pp. 48-49.
104 See ibid., pp. 42-43; Gray, "Circuit Diary, 1942-45"; and Gray interviews with C. Marshall, E.A. Fraser, Jacques Ste-Marie, Vaughn Deacon.
105 John Grierson, "A Film Policy for Canada," *Canadian Affairs*, June 14, 1944, p. 6.
106 Quoted in Gray, "Circuit Diary," 1944-45.
107 Ibid.
108 Maynard Collins, "Cooperation, Hollywood and Howe," *Cinema Canada*, June / July, 1979, pp. 34-36.

Chapter Nine: The Inevitable Denouement

1 Kirwan Cox, "The Grierson Files," *Cinema Canada*, June / July 1979, p. 18.
2 Al Sherman, "Grierson To Head State Department Film Unit," *Box Office*, April 14, 1945, cited in Cox, "The Grierson Files," p. 18.
3 Cox, "Grierson Files," p. 18.
4 Quoted in ibid.
5 Ibid., p. 17.
6 Quoted in ibid., p. 19.
7 Forsyth Hardy, ed., *Grierson On Documentary* (London: Faber & Faber, 1946), p. 117.
8 Forsyth Hardy, *John Grierson: A Documentary Biography* (London: Faber & Faber, 1979), p. 260.
9 Quoted in ibid., p. 261.
10 Quoted in ibid., pp. 105-106.
11 Quoted in ibid., p. 105.
12 See ibid., p. 153; and Cox, "Grierson Files," p. 19.
13 C.P. Stacey, *Canada and the Age of Conflict*, vol. 2: *1921-1948, The Mackenzie King Era* (Toronto: University of Toronto Press, 1981), p. 394.
14 Ibid.
15 Quoted in Gary Evans, *John Grierson and the National Film Board: The Politics of Wartime Propaganda* (Toronto: University of Toronto Press, 1984), p. 242.
16 Quoted in Hardy, *John Grierson*, p. 154.

17 Ibid., p. 155.
18 Ibid.
19 See especially Cox, "Grierson Files"; and Evans, *John Grierson and the* NFB, pp. 224-68.
20 Quoted in Cox, "Grierson Files," p. 19.
21 Quoted in ibid.
22 Ibid.
23 Ibid.
24 Quoted in Evans, *John Grierson and the* NFB, p. 253.
25 Ibid., p. 254.
26 Cox, "Grierson Files," pp. 21-22.
27 Peter Collier and David Horowitz, *The Rockefellers: An American Dynasty* (New York: Holt, Rinehart and Winston, 1976), pp. 234-48.
28 Elizabeth Sussex, *The Rise and Fall of British Documentary: The Story of the Film Movement Founded by John Grierson* (Berkeley: University of California Press, 1975), p. 103.
29 Hardy, *John Grierson,* p. 152. See also Cox, "Grierson Files," p. 19.
30 Cox, "Grierson Files," p. 22.
31 Ibid., p. 23.
32 Hardy, *John Grierson,* pp. 159-60.
33 Ibid., p. 162.
34 Cox, "Grierson Files," p. 20.
35 U.S. Department of State, "Freedom of the Press—World-wide," Bulletin no. 14, February 3, 1946, p. 160.
36 Ibid.
37 Hardy, *John Grierson,* p. 161.
38 Ibid.
39 Ibid.
40 Quoted in ibid.
41 Ibid., p. 162.
42 Cox, "Grierson Files," p. 22.
43 Ibid.
44 Quoted in ibid., p. 23.

Conclusion: The Hurricane of Change

1 Rodrigue Chiasson, "The CRTC Tapes," in The John Grierson Project–McGill University, eds., *John Grierson and the* NFB (Toronto: ECW Press, 1984), p. 44.
2 Forsyth Hardy, ed., *Grierson On Documentary* (London: Faber & Faber, 1946), pp. 131-32.
3 Gary Evans, *John Grierson and the National Film Board: The Politics of Wartime Propaganda* (Toronto: University of Toronto Press, 1984), p. 272.

4 Susan Crean, "Reading Between The Lies: Culture and the Free Trade Agreement," *This Magazine,* May 1988, p. 32.
5 Evans, *John Grierson and the* NFB, pp. 272-73.
6 Bertram Gross, *Friendly Fascism: The New Face of Power in America* (Montreal: Black Rose Books, 1980). pp. 32-53.
7 Edgar and Daphne Anstey, "Grierson as a Stimulator of Third-World Communications," in The John Grierson Project, *John Grierson and the* NFB, p. 7.

Index